Econometrics:

A Simple Introduction

Also by K.H. Erickson

Simple Introductions

Choice Theory
Econometrics
Financial Economics
Game Theory
Game Theory for Business
Investment Appraisal
Microeconomics

Econometrics:

A Simple Introduction

K.H. Erickson

Contents

Introduction to Econometrics

What exactly is econometrics? Like all branches of economics the field is designed to offer greater insight into the world around us, but econometrics is less concerned about theory and what should happen in a perfect world and more about what actually does happen in practice. The goal of econometrics is to understand the relationship between two (or more) variables, or in more simple terms to understand the cause of changes in real world variables. For example, the focus may be an examination of the factors affecting demand for a particular product, which would be of great concern to any business hoping to increase their sales. Or the analysis may look into the relationship between education level and salary, a topic of interest to those considering additional learning and certification.

The field being investigated for its determinants (e.g. product demand and sales, or salary income) is known as the dependent or y variable, and the issue being assessed as a possible cause (e.g. a product's price, or education and certification level) is the independent or x variable. For every possible level of the independent x variable there will be a corresponding amount for the dependent y variable, as the following diagram example suggests.

Independent and dependent variables

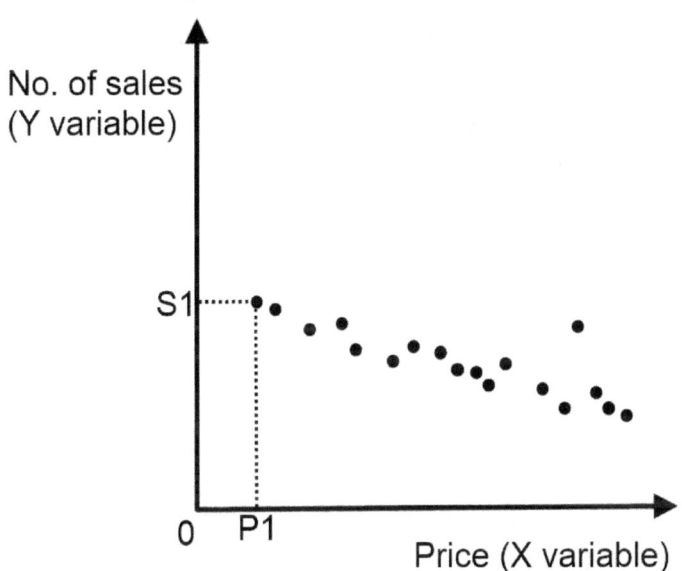

The diagram shows different levels of a product's price and the number of sales that may result, with the various black dots giving the relationship between the two. At price P1 there are S1 sales and every other price level will have its own level of demand and sales too. The information here shows a general negative relationship between price and sales, with higher prices linked with lower numbers of sales.

However, there will never be a definitive answer to the relationship between two variables, and there are always exceptions to any trend or rule. While a lower price may encourage higher product demand and sales there will be consumers who will buy a product no matter what the price. And although greater education and certification may be linked with a higher salary there are exceptions, with some people with little or no education still able to secure a well-paid job. The next diagram shows the overall trend between a hypothetical product's price and the number of sales, known as a best fit line, with attention also drawn to an outlier that bucks the trend and is noticeably separate from this trend line.

Best fit line

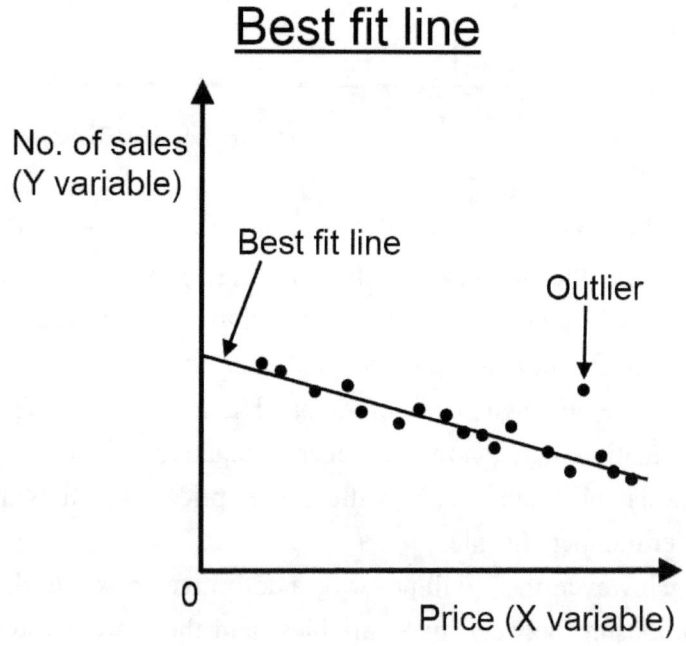

The presence of a single outlier is noteworthy but it doesn't affect the overall trend here, and the negative relationship between price and number of sales remains the most important feature. The best fit or trend line allows for predictions to be made for other values of price and sales not shown in the diagram, which is helpful for a business wanting to know the sales to expect for a certain price level and prepare their stock supply accordingly. In alternative scenarios with different variables under consideration it could show the likely returns to greater education, and in a more general sense the best fit line supports a greater understanding of cause and effect.

Econometrics essentially revolves around finding the best fit line giving the relationship between two variables, and this requires three pieces of information. First there is the intercept or constant, which is the point where the best fit line cuts the y axis of the y or dependent variable. The value of the intercept is usually symbolized with the Greek letter alpha, α. A second factor determining the best fit line is its slope, which may be positive and upward sloping or negative and downward sloping, and it may range from the horizontal to the vertical. The value of the best fit line's slope can be symbolized with the Greek letter beta, β. Finally, there is the degree of error linked with the best fit line, which shows how far the actual dependent variable data points are from the best fit line on average, represented by the Greek letter epsilon, ε.

An equation can summarize the relationship between the different factors, known as the linear regression model:

$$y = \alpha + \beta x + \varepsilon$$

Y is the dependent variable (e.g. no. of sales here), and it equals the value of the intercept, added to the value of beta multiplied by the level of the independent x variable (e.g. a product's price), plus the size of the vertical error term. Another diagram can make the model clearer and illustrate the intercept, slope and error in greater depth.

Intercept, slope and error

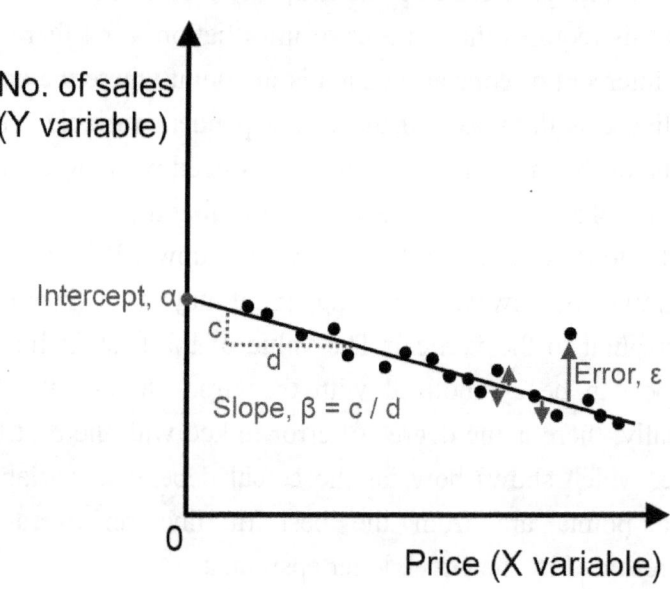

The intercept is the starting point for the relationship between a product's price and its sales, and the slope begins at this point and represents how a change in the x variable (d) affects a change in the y variable (c). Dividing the value of c by the value of d will give the slope or beta coefficient, and c will be negative for a downward sloping line (as here) and positive for an upward sloping line. Finally, the error term gives the average deviation of a data point from the best fit line, and while an outlier may lie far from the trend line the data points closer to it will reduce the average overall error found with the best fit line. Minimizing the error in the model to find the most accurate best fit line is the biggest challenge in econometrics, and this is the subject of the next section.

Best Linear Unbiased Estimators (BLUE)

The starting point to minimize the error in a linear regression model is with the ordinary least squares (OLS) method. This squares (^{2}) the value of each individual error (εi) where a data point deviates from the best fit line, in order to remove the negative sign of some error values to make deviations above and below the trend line equivalent and comparable. With all individual data errors in the same format the OLS method simply sums ($\sum$) them all and then selects the model with the lowest or minimum (min) amount of predicted error, using estimates for alpha ($\underline{\alpha}$) and beta ($\underline{\beta}$):

$$\text{Min}_{\underline{\alpha},\underline{\beta}} \sum \underline{\varepsilon} i^2$$

The alpha and beta estimates are based on:

$$\underline{\beta} = \sum xiyi / \sum xi^2$$
$$\underline{\alpha} = \cancel{Y} - \underline{\beta}\cancel{X}$$

Here xi = Xi - $\cancel{X}$, and xi represents an individual value from the overall independent data population of interest (e.g. one possible value of a product's price), Xi an individual value of the limited data sample that is acting as a proxy for the complete population data set (e.g. one of fifty product prices used in a sample), and X̶ is the sample mean. Similarly, yi = Yi - Y̶, and yi represents an individual value from the dependent data population of interest (e.g. a possible number of sales), Yi one result from the limited data sample, and Y̶ the sample mean.

The OLS method removes those models which include avoidable error and focuses in on the one model (i.e. best fit line) with only unavoidable levels of error, to offer the best prediction and approximation of the actual points in the dataset. With a perfect model the predicted individual values (y̲i) would always equal the actual individual values (yi), but this isn't possible due to variation in the data points which sees individual points differ from the mean average (y̶). Note that y̲ is simply y underlined, representing an estimation in this book, while y̶ is y with a strike through it, to show the mean average. The letter i represents individual values, in place of average values.

The total sum of squares (TSS) gives the total variation in the dataset, and it squares the difference between each actual data point (yi) and the actual mean average (y̶) to make variations above and below the mean equivalent, and then sums them to reveal the TSS:

$$\text{TSS} = \sum(yi - \bar{y})^2$$

13

The explained sum of squares (ESS) gives the variation between the predictions made by the model and the actual data, as it squares the difference between each estimated data point ($\underline{y}i$) and the actual mean average ($\bar{y}$) to make variations above and below the mean equivalent, before summing them to give the ESS:

$$ESS = \sum(\underline{y}i - \bar{y})^2$$

TSS - ESS = RSS, the residual sum of squares. This gives the variation between the actual and predicted data, squaring the difference between each actual data point (yi) and each estimated data point ($\underline{y}i$) for the reasons noted above, before summing them all for the RSS result:

$$RSS = \sum(yi - \underline{y}i)^2 = \sum\underline{\varepsilon}i^2$$

R^2, the coefficient of determination, shows the accuracy of a model and ranges from 0 (completely inaccurate) to 1 (perfect). It can be found with the TSS value and either the ESS or the RSS:

$$R^2 = (ESS / TSS)$$
$$R^2 = 1 - (RSS / TSS)$$

A superior model should have a low RSS and a high R^2 value, and be efficient, consistent, unbiased and sufficient, and the Gauss-Markov theorem gives the conditions for this Best Linear Unbiased Estimator (BLUE). For an unbiased estimator two conditions are required:

1. The x variables are fixed on repeated sampling;
2. Expected individual error is zero, $E(\varepsilon i) = 0$.

The first of these two conditions means that the causation in the model goes in one direction, from the x variable (e.g. price) to the y variable (e.g. number of sales), and no matter how many times the model is run changes in the dependent y variable do not change the x variable which remains fixed. The second condition is an obvious one, where the expected level of error is zero and all error is random. This makes intuitive sense and if the variations are expected then they aren't error at all, and they simply represent a factor that needs to be accounted for in an improved model.

For a linear model the functional form must also be linear. This means that there must be an independent variable that can be changed as desired and not limited by codependency with different factors, unlike with $y = \alpha k \beta l$ where k and l factors are multiplied by each other and a change in one will affect the impact of the other. Instead the model must follow a separate form such as $y = \alpha k + \beta l$ where the individual effects of k and l can be recorded.

This condition is naturally met with the use of the linear regression model noted above: $y = \alpha + \beta x + \varepsilon$.

All that is left for the model to be BLUE is for it to be the best and most efficient model with the lowest variance, and this depends upon two further conditions:

3. Homoscedasticity or constant variance, $E(\varepsilon i^2) = \sigma^2$;
4. No autocorrelation, cov $(\varepsilon i, \varepsilon j) = 0$ with $i \neq j$.

Homoscedasticity means all random variables in the data sequence have the same finite variance (σ^2, which is standard deviation, σ, squared to make positive and negative deviations equivalent). This is the opposite situation to heteroscedasticity where there's changing variance through the sample and the variance depends upon the value of the x variable, suggesting the model is flawed and changes need to be made to account for the additional error that appears with certain values of x.

No autocorrelation depends upon errors remaining unrelated to each other with no covariance (cov). Unrelated error eliminates the risk of random error found in one item of data spreading to another due to correlation, and this will reduce the variance and error in a data sample.

Hypothesis Testing

Once a BLUE regression model has been found it can be used to analyse data and form conclusions. But there is one further condition required of a model to use it in a regression and test a hypothesis:

5. Error is normally distributed, $\varepsilon \sim N(0, \sigma^2)$

This means the error distribution has a mean of zero and variance of σ^2 as would be expected. It follows a bell curve shape, with most values close to the mean, all values falling within a certain range, and an equal likelihood of an error value being above zero as below it. Error and variance must be normally distributed in order for the data estimates, which will naturally contain some unavoidable error, to be likewise. And the data estimates must be normally distributed in order to be tested with a hypothesis and assessed against a set standard for their accuracy.

With this assumption met the process of hypothesis testing can proceed, and it involves the following steps:

1) State the hypothesis;
2) Identify the test statistic and its distribution;
3) State the significance level and decision rule;

4) Collect and calculate the required data;
5) Determine the statistical and economic results.

1) Stating the hypothesis will come from the economic question of interest, and the process involves putting forward a null hypothesis (H0) where an independent parameter is said to have a certain value, for example:

$$H0: \beta = 0$$
$$H0: \beta = 2$$

An alternative hypothesis (H1) which contradicts the null hypothesis is always put forward with it, for example:

$$H1: \beta \neq 0$$
$$H1: \beta \neq 2$$

There is a two-tailed hypothesis test when the null H0 hypothesis takes the form '=' and H1 the form '$\neq$' as here, and this is typically the method to use as it examines deviations both above and below the predicated value. But if the H1 hypothesis tests in only one direction, such as H1: $\beta > 0$, this involves a one-tailed (one-sided) test. A hypothesis test often tests if a variable is significant or insignificant and equal to zero, and therefore irrelevant in a model. It typically takes the form H0: $\beta = 0$, and H1: $\beta \neq$

0 to assess an x variable, and H0: $\alpha = 0$, H1: $\alpha \neq 0$ to assess the constant term.

2) Identification of the test distribution and test statistic depends upon the data being evaluated. Some distributions and their test statistic methods assume a small number of observations or only one independent x variable, while others are designed for larger amounts of data or multiple x variables, and a model may require for the error and variance to be known or it may function with an estimate. The various types of test available will be explained as needed later in this book.

3) The significance level (SL) (or alpha (α) level, while the confidence level is 1 - SL) in a hypothesis test gives the percentage margin of error that is accepted, where random chance is thought unlikely to explain the result. There are four possible results in any test:

Reject H0 correctly;
Reject H0 incorrectly (type I error);
Fail to reject H0 correctly;
Fail to reject H0 incorrectly (type II error).

The probability of type I error is the significance level (SL), α, and the probability of type II error is β. The SL will be chosen in advance before the test is run and a 5% level is a typical choice, which can see results incorrect 5% of the time. A smaller significance level such as 1%

may seem appealing, but due to the inevitable error in any model this may see all models fail the test despite being good enough to predict actual results most of the time.

With the SL chosen the critical value for what the data values should be can be found in statistical tables. A 5% significance level (95% confidence level) may give a value such as 1.99, while a more stringent 1% level could give a higher value such as 2.62, for a critical region of $\pm$ 1.99 and $\pm$ 2.62 respectively. If the value calculated with the test statistic is outside this region then the null hypothesis is rejected, but we fail to reject the null hypothesis if it's within this region. Note that the null hypothesis is never accepted, and we can only reject or fail to reject it.

4) Collecting and calculating the data is the next step but first an estimator is required to proxy the population data's variance (σ^2) and its sample distribution, which is unknown. An unbiased estimator of the variance is:

$$\underline{\sigma}^2 = \sum \underline{\varepsilon}i^2 / (n - 2)$$

This says that the estimated variance (underlined $\underline{\sigma}^2$) equals the residual sum of squares (RSS = $\sum \underline{\varepsilon}i^2$) divided by the degrees of freedom (DF) of n - 2. The degrees of freedom equals the number of observations in the sample (n) minus the number of variables in the model (2 here). If the error ε is distributed normally (as assumed earlier) then the following can be shown on repeated sampling:

20

$$(n - 2)\,\underline{\sigma}^2 / \sigma^2 \sim \chi^2_{(n-2)}$$

The degrees of freedom multiplied by the estimated variance, with the result divided by the actual variance, approximately follows a Chi-squared distribution χ^2. The ratio of a standard normal distribution to the square root of an augmented χ^2 distribution is the t distribution with the same degrees of freedom as the Chi-squared distribution (e.g. n - 2). If sample variance $\underline{\sigma}^2$ is used as the estimator then on repeated sampling the following holds, where $\underline{Se}(\beta)$ is the estimated (sample) standard error (Se) of $\underline{\beta}$:

$$(\underline{\beta} - \beta) / \underline{Se}(\underline{\beta}) \sim t_{(n-2)}$$

This result allows for hypothesis tests to be run on β (and the intercept α in a similar way) without requiring knowledge of the actual population parameters. If the null hypothesis, H0, was $\beta = 0$ then this result will simplify to:

$$\underline{\beta} / \underline{Se}(\underline{\beta}) \sim t_{(n-2)}$$

And if H0: $\beta = 2$ then the result will simplify to:

$$\underline{\beta} - 2 / \underline{Se}(\underline{\beta}) \sim t_{(n-2)}$$

The formula for the beta estimate, $\underline{\beta}$, was given earlier (with alpha estimate $\underline{\alpha}$) and only the estimated variance of the sample beta, var(β), is needed (and sample alpha, var(α), to test on α). The sample beta variance estimate is:

$$\underline{var}(\beta) = \underline{\sigma}^2 / \sum xi^2$$

And the estimated variance for the sample alpha is:

$$\underline{var}(\alpha) = \underline{\sigma}^2 / (\sum Xi^2 / n\sum xi^2)$$

These results could be calculated by hand but there's an easier way, and the data can be put into software to perform a regression. This can be done in Microsoft Excel and with the Analysis Toolpak as an Add-in it's simply a case of selecting the Data tab, then Data Analysis, then Regression, before inputting the independent x value data column and dependent y value data column separately.

The sample data here comes from 16 paired observations, where x gives the quarterly rate of unemployment in South East England over the years 1975-78 (Department of Employment Gazette), and y is the proportionate rate of change in the Retail Price Index, a national UK inflation measure, over the same period (Economic Trends Annual Supplement). The 1975-78 period saw huge changes in inflation and possible causes are worth investigation, with unemployment an intuitively obvious one as if people don't have jobs they won't have money to spend to push up prices.

(1) y = 20.35, x = 2.0;
(2) y = 24.34, x = 2.5;
(3) y = 26.56, x = 2.8;
(4) y = 25.29, x = 3.4;
(5) y = 22.54, x = 3.7;
(6) y = 15.94, x = 3.9;
(7) y = 13.73, x = 4.0;
(8) y = 14.95, x = 4.0;
(9) y = 16.50, x = 4.1;
(10) y = 17.41, x = 4.1;
(11) y = 16.50, x = 4.2;
(12) y = 13.01, x = 4.2;
(13) y = 9.44, x = 4.0;
(14) y = 7.71, x = 3.9;
(15) y = 7.88, x = 3.8;
(16) y = 8.13, x = 3.6.

This sample data gives various results after a regression is performed, with the more important statistics represented below:

Regression Statistics
R square = 0.32114

Residual
SS = 397.296
MS = 28.378

Coefficients
Intercept = 36.045
X variable 1 = -5.4371

Standard Error
Intercept = 7.7997
X variable 1 = 2.1128

t Stat
Intercept = 4.6213
X variable 1 = -2.5735

P-value
Intercept = 0.000396
X variable 1 = 0.022088

In this example R square (R^2) equals 0.321, and this suggests the intercept and x variable explain only about 32% of the changes in the dependent y variable.

The unexplained residual sum of squares (RSS) and error is 397.296, and dividing this by the degrees of freedom (n - 2 = 14) gives the MS residual or the mean squared error of the estimator ($\underline{\sigma^2}$), at 28.378. This sample value here acts as a proxy for the true population variance, σ^2, though it may have limited use due to only 16 sample observations. Taking the square root of the MS value gives standard deviation of $\underline{\sigma}$ = 5.327, and this is how far each of the y variable data observations here lies from the best fit line on average, either above or below it.

The best fit line which defines the model is determined by the intercept and x variable 1 (slope) coefficients, the alpha and beta estimates respectively, and $\underline{\alpha}$ = 36.045 while $\underline{\beta}$ = -5.4371. The standard error for the intercept and X variable 1 are the Se for alpha and beta respectively, and $\underline{Se}(\underline{\alpha})$ = 7.7997 while $\underline{Se}(\underline{\beta})$ = 2.1128. These values can be put into the formula given earlier when H0: β = 0 or H0: α = 0, for the test result:

$$\beta / \underline{Se}(\beta) \sim t_{(n-2)}$$
$$-2.5734 \sim t_{(n-2)}$$

And the same can be done for the intercept, α:

$$\alpha / \underline{Se}(\alpha) \sim t_{(n-2)}$$
$$4.6213 \sim t_{(n-2)}$$

This data, or values slightly different due to rounding, is found without requiring these calculations in the t Stat results above. But it's useful to understand the calculation method just used in case the t Stat isn't available.

5) The data result is compared to the 5% significance level (SL) critical value, for n - 2 = 14 observations, to assess the test. The critical value is $\pm$ 2.145 and because both the intercept and x variable results of 4.62 and -2.57

are above the critical value we reject the two null hypotheses, H0: β = 0, and H0: α = 0. This last step could be done without calculations or tables by looking at the P-value data above and comparing it to the SL, and if the p-value is lower the null hypothesis is rejected. Because the significance level of 5% or 0.05 is above the intercept p-value of 0.000396 and X variable 1 p-value of 0.022088 both null hypotheses are rejected. But the p-value (also known as t-prob or unnamed in brackets in regression results) may not always be known, and it's useful to know how to test a hypothesis without it.

Rejecting the null hypothesis that alpha and beta factors are zero is the statistical result, but finding meaning in this is the economic result. Sample results reject the idea that the factors are insignificant and irrelevant with zero effect, and both a constant factor and unemployment appear significant and may play a role in explaining the inflation rate over 1975-8 in SE England. The very low p-value for the intercept suggests that a constant factor (i.e. a trend) is especially likely to hold influence in inflation. A prediction can be made of the value of the y variable here (inflation) with only the knowledge of the x variable (unemployment), and the estimated economic relationship found is as follows:

$$\underline{y}i = 36.045 - 5.437x$$

Multiple Regression

The linear model examined so far has been very simple in terms of the functional form and only a single x variable:

$$y = \alpha + \beta x + \varepsilon$$

But using only one explanatory factor and the simplest functional form limits a regression model, and in practice the analysis requires examination of multiple independent x variables, and the model may require different forms. In terms of alternative functional forms, there may be times when the range of data for a variable is significantly wide that it can cause problems when trying to analyse results. To make a large range of data more manageable a typical solution is to take natural logs (ln, or log to base e) of the variable of concern, for example:

$$y = \alpha + \beta \, Ln \, (x) + \varepsilon$$
$$Ln \, (y) = \alpha + \beta x + \varepsilon$$
$$Ln \, (y) = \alpha + \beta \, Ln \, (x) + \varepsilon$$

The first equation is known as linear-log (the left side of the equation is linear, the right side logarithmic), the second equation log-linear, and the third log-log. One single regression won't always be enough to tell the whole story, and even with a limited data range it can be useful to run multiple separate regressions with both log and linear forms for a comparison. However, although linear form x variables can be compared with a model with log form x variables, the form of the y variable must remain constant as yi and Ln (yi) form models can't be compared.

A more common method to conduct multiple regression analysis is not to run one regression after another but to use a model that contains multiple x variables together. The total number of independent variables used, all x variables and the error variable, is usually represented by the letter k, and that creates the following linear multiple regression equation:

$$y = \alpha + \beta_1 x_1 + \ldots + \beta_{k-1} x_{k-1} + \varepsilon$$

And the OLS estimator changes accordingly:

$$\text{Min}_{\alpha, \beta_1, \ldots, \beta_{k-1}} \sum \varepsilon_i^2$$

One new condition is required to test the multiple regression model with OLS, for the sixth condition overall:

6. There is no exact linear relationship (perfect multicollinearity) between any of the explanatory independent variables.

All of the other assumptions remain from earlier for the reasons already given. As before an unbiased estimator, $\underline{\sigma^2}$, is required for the population variance, σ^2, and this uses the same formula as before with the residual sum of squares (RSS) divided by the number of degrees of freedom in the regression (n - k):

$$\underline{\sigma^2} = \sum \underline{\varepsilon} i^2 / (n - k) = RSS / (n - k)$$

N is the number of observations and k the number of expected parameters here. This is exactly the same equation as given earlier for a single x variable model, except that a k replaces the 2 that was used previously as in this model k won't always equal 2 and can take any number of values.

Testing a hypothesis about an individual parameter in a multiple regression model follows the same formula as with the single x variable model, except that k replaces 2 as noted, and the coefficient for the variable in question must be identified. For example, in a one x variable model it was H0: $\beta = 0$, H1: $\beta \neq 0$ to test if the parameter was significant or not, and H0: $\beta = 2$, H1: $\beta \neq 2$ to test if the x variable had a specific impact of a factor of 2. But in a multiple x variable model where parameter x3 was the one tested these examples would become H0: $\beta 3 = 0$, H1: $\beta 3 \neq 0$, and H0: $\beta 3 = 2$, H1: $\beta 3 \neq 2$, with the following test:

$$(\underline{\beta3} - \beta3) / \underline{Se}(\beta3) \sim t_{(n-k)}$$

A multiple variable regression also allows for population variances to be compared, $\sigma1^2 = \sigma2^2$, as a model can be run with and without certain variables to see how this affects the variance. This would use two estimators, $\underline{\sigma1^2}$ and $\underline{\sigma2^2}$, from independent data samples drawn from normally distributed populations. With these assumptions the following holds on repeated sampling:

$$(\underline{\sigma1^2} / \sigma1^2) / (\underline{\sigma2^2} / \sigma2^2) \sim F_{df1, df2}$$

The F stands for an F distribution, which is a ratio of two augmented χ distributions (while the t distribution used earlier for a test statistic was a ratio to the square root of one augmented χ distribution). An F test can be used for two different purposes, the first of which is to test the significance of all variables in a multiple regression model together, to test if a model is completely worthless:

$$H0: \beta_1 = \beta_2 = \ldots = \beta_{k-1} = 0$$
$$H1: \text{Not all variables equal zero (at least one} \neq 0)$$

This hypothesis's test statistic follows, where TSS is the total sum of squares, RSS the residual sum of squares:

$$F = [(TSS - RSS) / k - 1] / [RSS / n - k]$$

The second part of this equation, [RSS / n - k], is always an unbiased estimator of the population variance, $\underline{\sigma}^2$, and the first part of the formula, [(TSS - RSS) / k - 1], is also an unbiased estimator if the null hypothesis is true and all variables are insignificant. On repeated sampling the distribution of the test statistic is $F_{df1, df2} = F_{n-k, k-1}$ here, but if the null hypothesis is rejected and not all parameters equal zero then the test statistic will be biased upwards. This means there's no chance of rejecting the null on the left (less than negative critical value) side, and the reject or fail to decision for the F test is based on the right hand tail of the test statistic (more than positive critical value).

An R^2 goodness of fit measure ($R^2 = 1 - (RSS/TSS)$) will be biased upwards with more independent variables used in a model, no matter if the variables are irrelevant or not. This will give a poor indication of a model's true accuracy but an adjusted R^2 measure, aR^2, can compensate and accounts for the number of independent variables:

$$aR^2 = [1 - (1 - R^2)] \times [(n - 1) / (n - k)]$$

The F test given above may now be rewritten in terms of R^2, and the new formula will have the same F distribution properties as before. This allows it to accurately test a null hypothesis that R^2 equals zero, and none of the independent variables can explain changes in the dependent variable as they all equal zero:

31

$$F = [R^2 / k] / [(1 - R^2) / n - k - 1]$$

A second function of the F test is to test the significance of additional variables in a model. This is important as including irrelevant additional variables will create inefficiency in the estimators, while not including relevant additional variables will create bias. A test can determine if additional variables need to be included or excluded, and this divides a model into two separate versions, with a full unrestricted version with all variables and a restricted version which removes some variables. A restricted model may look as follows, where the x variables begin with x_1 and end with x_m:

$$yi = \alpha + \beta_1 x_{1i} + \ldots + \beta_m x_{mi} + \varepsilon i$$

And an unrestricted model may add x_{m+1}, x_{m+2} and so on until a final x variable of x_{k-1}, where the removed restriction, $r = k - 1 - m$:

$$yi = \alpha + \beta_1 x_{1i} + \ldots + \beta_m x_{mi} + \beta_{m+1} x_{m+1i} + \beta_{m+2} x_{m+2i} + \ldots + \beta_{k-1} x_{k-1i} + \varepsilon i$$

A test can examine if the additional r variables make a significant difference to the model, with the null hypothesis that they don't as they equal zero:

$$H0: \beta_{m+1} = \beta_{m+2} = \ldots = \beta_{k-1} = 0$$
H1: Not all r variables equal zero

An unbiased estimator of σ^2 can be found with the unrestricted model, based upon the residual sum of squares (RSS) of the unrestricted model (uRSS):

$$uRSS / n - k$$

If the null hypothesis H0 is true and all r variables equal zero then the additional reduction in the RSS and increase in R^2 is due to statistical error. A further unbiased estimator will then be as follows, where rRSS is the restricted model RSS, and r the number of variables represented by the restriction:

$$rRSS - uRSS / r$$

This will be an upwardly biased estimator of σ^2 if the null hypothesis is untrue and the r variables don't equal zero, to give the following test statistic where k is the number of estimated parameters in the unrestricted model:

$$F = [(rRSS - uRSS) / r] / [uRSS / n - k]$$

As before the distribution of the F test statistic under H0 on repeated sampling is $F_{df1, df2}$, and here this equals F_r,

$n-k$ as could be predicted by looking at the numerator and denominator. The F test statistic may also be adapted to:

$$F = [(R^2_U - R^2_R) / r] / [(1 - R^2_U) / n - k]$$

Where R^2_U is the R^2 for the unrestricted model, and R^2_R is the R^2 for the restricted model. The test can be generalized to evaluate any set of linear restrictions.

The F test is an important tool even if t tests have already suggested that individual variables are all insignificant, and an F test may find the opposite result in a multiple regression model. The cause is highly correlated independent variables (but not perfectly correlated, to ensure condition 6. No perfect multicollinearity is not violated), and this increases the variance of the estimators and reduces their precision, as error in one variable spreads to another. This causes a need for a greater confidence (lower significance) level and gives a tendency to fail to reject the F test null hypothesis that all variables equal zero. This phenomenon is often found when variables matter as a group but their effect can't be separated with precision, i.e. variables are complements.

Dummy Variables

The previous analysis has aimed to find the value of the beta coefficient variables, β_1, $\beta_2 \ldots \beta_{k-1}$, in order to understand the effect that the corresponding independent parameter, x_1, $x_2 \ldots x_{k-1}$, has on the dependent parameter being assessed, y. But it has been assumed that the true population beta value being estimated is constant across all observations (e.g. a 1 unit change in x always gives a 1.7 unit change in y), and that any deviation from it in individual observations is due to unavoidable variance and error, which we have looked to minimize. However, it may not necessarily be the case that the effect of x on y is constant across all observations, and while this may hold with quantitative factors it may not with more qualitative data such as when describing the characteristics of people.

A multiple regression model can be extended to represent scenarios where the parameters differ for some or all of the sample observations. This process uses dummy variables, explanatory variables which may take only a limited number of possible values (typically 0 and 1) in order to model a situation with only two possible outcomes.

An intercept dummy variable can be used in cases where the qualitative data changes the value of the intercept or constant in a regression model. For example, the price of a house Pi (dependent y variable) may depend only upon the size of the house Si in square feet (independent x variable) as in the following equation:

$$Pi = \alpha + \beta Si + \varepsilon i$$

However, the effect that the size of a house has upon its price is unlikely to be the same across all sample observations, and those homes in more desirable neighbourhoods will add a premium to the cost. If this premium is fixed the intercept dummy variable models it as follows:

D = 1, if house is in desirable neighbourhood
D = 0, if house is not in desirable neighbourhood

If Di is added to the equation for house prices above, with the new parameter δ, the result becomes:

$$Pi = \alpha + \delta Di + \beta Si + \varepsilon i$$

And the estimated (E) relationship will depend on whether or not the house is in a desirable neighbourhood and if the value of the intercept dummy is 1 or 0, as the intercept dummy may create a parallel shift in the relationship between house price and size to the value of δ:

$$\text{If } D = 1 \text{ then (E) Pi} = (\alpha + \delta) + \beta Si$$
$$\text{If } D = 0 \text{ then (E) Pi} = \alpha + \beta Si$$

A second type of dummy variable is a slope dummy. This is used where the qualitative data changes the relationship in a non-fixed way, and a new variable needs to be added that is the product of a continuous variable and a dummy variable. For example, perhaps being in a desirable neighbourhood doesn't simply add a constant fixed premium to the price of a house (e.g. 50,000 more on every house price), but instead the premium depends on the size of the house in square feet (e.g. 100 added for every additional square foot). This can be modelled with a slope dummy or interaction variable SiDi, the product of the house size and the dummy, and a new parameter γ:

$$Pi = \alpha + \beta Si + \gamma(SiDi) + \varepsilon i$$

The interaction variable equals the value of house size when the home is in a desirable neighbourhood and $D = 1$, and is zero for the other houses situated in undesirable neighbourhoods where $D = 0$. This creates the following expectations (E) for house price:

$$\text{If } D = 1 \text{ then (E) Pi} = \alpha + (\beta + \gamma)Si$$
$$\text{If } D = 0 \text{ then (E) Pi} = \alpha + \beta Si$$

The price of a home per square foot in a desirable neighbourhood is ($\beta + \gamma$), and in other less desirable locations the price per square foot is β, with any changes in house size affecting the price by this amount respectively. A hypothesis can test whether or not the desirability of a house's location affects the price per square foot, and the null hypothesis would be that it doesn't matter while the alternative hypothesis would be that the area makes a difference to price:

$$H0: \gamma = 0$$
$$H1: \gamma \neq 0$$

Or to make the t test more specific the alternative hypothesis could be that the more desirable area raises the price, as that's what is expected to be found in the data:

$$H0: \gamma = 0$$
$$H1: \gamma > 0$$

In practice however neither of the two situations modelled so far describe the effect that a more desirable neighbourhood will have on a house's price. It's not usually the case that a better area adds a fixed amount to price, which remains the same with both small and large homes. But it would also be unusual to see a house price increase at a constant rate no matter the number of square feet involved, and when a large quantity of anything is bought there is typically a discount. A house's price would be expected to rise with size, as with the slope dummy, but the relative impact of house size on price should decrease as the number of square feet rises, as with the intercept dummy where the constant factor will dominate the equation except with larger house sizes. In simple terms the effect of a desirable neighbourhood on price requires both an intercept and an interaction dummy variable:

$$Pi = \alpha + \delta Di + \beta Si + \gamma(SiDi) + \varepsilon i$$

And the expected (E) price can be given for both a desirable neighbourhood where $D = 1$, and an undesirable neighbourhood where $D = 0$:

$$\text{If } D = 1 \text{ then (E) } Pi = (\alpha + \delta) + (\beta + \gamma)Si$$
$$\text{If } D = 0 \text{ then (E) } Pi = \alpha + \beta Si$$

This example uses one neighbourhood desirability dummy twice in the regression model, but the analysis can be expanded to use several different dummies together. A wage equation may be estimated where an individual worker's wages are thought to be a function of factors relating to productivity, and when assessing such equations it's customary to also include dummies for race and sex, to examine how different groups of workers are performing and how they're rewarded. But including only race and sex dummies doesn't note the effects of interactions between the two, such as for a white male worker or non-white female worker, and a combined race multiplied by sex variable is also required. The following wage (W) equation accounts for this, and it simplifies the analysis by using only worker experience (EX) as a single productivity measure:

$$W = \alpha + \beta EX + \delta_1 RACE + \delta_2 SEX + \gamma(RACE \times SEX) + \varepsilon$$

In this equation δ_1 and δ_2 are the parameters for the race and sex intercept dummies respectively, while γ is again the parameter for an interaction or slope dummy and here it represents the combination of race and sex. The race and sex dummies operate as follows:

RACE = 1: White
RACE = 0: Non-white
SEX = 1: Male
SEX = 0: Female

δ_1 measures the effect that being white has on wages, δ_2 measures the effect of being male, γ measures the effect of being a white male, and others are compared to these categories. These dummies give the following expected wage, (E) W, for a white male, white female, non-white male, and non-white female accordingly:

$$\text{White male: (E) W} = (\alpha + \delta_1 + \delta_2 + \gamma) + \beta EX$$
$$\text{White female: (E) W} = (\alpha + \delta_1) + \beta EX$$
$$\text{Non-white male: (E) W} = (\alpha + \delta_2) + \beta EX$$
$$\text{Non-white female: (E) W} = \alpha + \beta EX$$

However, there will also be situations where the qualitative factor in question has more than two possible categories, for example with regions of a country, or an individual's level of educational attainment. In order to represent these situations a separate binary dummy needs to be created for every possible option in a category, where a 1 represents that the factor is present, and a 0 that it isn't. The next example looks again at a wage equation but this time focuses on the productivity side of things, with a variable for experience and a range of dummies for each level of education achievement, which proxies for skill.

The education dummies represent 4 possibilities: E_0, no formal qualifications; E_1, completed high school; E_2, bachelor's degree; E_3, postgraduate degree:

$$W = \alpha + \beta EX + \delta_1 E_1 + \delta_2 E_2 + \delta_3 E_3 + \varepsilon$$

Note that not all of the dummies for educational attainment have been included, and E_0, no formal qualifications, has been deliberately left out. If it wasn't then exact collinearity would exist, violating condition 6 required for a multiple regression model, as the sum of all education categories will be one to create an intercept variable which is an exact linear combination of the education dummies. This situation is known as the 'dummy variable trap', and if the dummy category is exhaustive where all of the category dummies sum to one then the usual solution is to remove one category, which then serves as the reference group others are compared to. The expected wage (E) W based on education level is:

No formal qualifications: (E) $W = \alpha + \beta EX$
Completed high school: (E) $W = (\alpha + \delta_1) + \beta EX$
Bachelor's degree: (E) $W = (\alpha + \delta_2) + \beta EX$
Postgraduate degree: (E) $W = (\alpha + \delta_3) + \beta EX$

The intercept parameter α represents the base wage for a worker with no qualifications and no experience, and with experience parameter β added this gives the wage for an experienced but unqualified person. Parameter δ_1 shows the expected wage differential between those with no formal qualifications and those who completed high school, parameter δ_2 between those with no qualifications and people with a bachelor's degree, and so on. And the relative comparison can be changed by leaving out a different dummy, shifting one of the δ to E_0.

While the dummy variables to include in a wage equation may be relatively obvious, in other scenarios some thought may need to be given to the dummies to be added to a model, and any type of dummy may be included if it's felt it will add insight. For example, in a model that seeks to explain the number of units of ice cream sold it would make sense to add seasonal dummies, as sales are unlikely to be the same throughout the year and higher demand would be expected in the hotter summer months. The seasonal dummies could divide the year into four quarters of spring, summer, autumn and winter, or alternatively a dummy could be created for all twelve of the calendar months, with a 1 value given when it's that season or month and a 0 otherwise. But either way not all of the months or seasons can have dummies to ensure the exact collinearity problem is avoided.

In a business model that examines weekly or monthly price or income data over many years it's often common to see annual dummies, and this can capture effects that may otherwise be missed. National economies will often follow a business cycle of growth periods and recessions, and annual dummies for specific individual years noted for significant upturns or downturns can determine if changes in prices can be attributed to independent variables, or if they're only due to a broader business cycle trend.

Periods of longer-run structural adjustment in the economic environment should also be taken into account with dummies, and so called 'regime changes' should be isolated accordingly. For example, the years where a country is at war will show different trends to peacetime, and any economic analysis of Western Europe in the 20th century should include dummies for the years 1914-18 and 1939-45, the periods of the two world wars. And macroeconomic consumption analysis should note the long-run changes brought about by the OPEC crisis of 1973, and a time dummy may be used to give a $D = 1$ to the years before this, and a $D = 0$ for the years after it. In terms of more recent economic structure changes any economic analysis of recent decades should include a dummy which separates the period from 2007 onwards, with the financial crisis and the global recession which has followed, as this period has been distinctly different from the years which preceded it.

It's very simple to include the data on dummies into a regression model in Excel, and each dummy variable (e.g. RACE, SEX, RACE x SEX, etc.) should have its own column next to other independent variables, with a 1 or 0 in the cell in each row according to the qualitative data linked with an observation. When the data is selected in the regression model the dependent data values (e.g. wage) is selected as the y variable, while all of the independent data values (e.g. experience, race dummy, sex dummy, race x sex dummy) are selected together as the x variable.

Chow Tests

The following diagram takes another look at house prices for both desirable and undesirable neighbourhoods. A certain data relationship may be found between house price and house size in each type of area, and the two best fit lines below represent theoretical regression equations.

Undesirable and desirable neighbourhood comparison

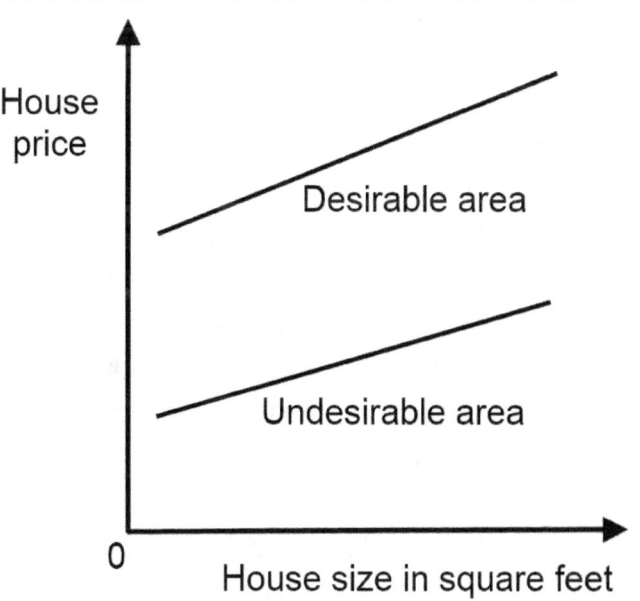

House price

Desirable area

Undesirable area

0

House size in square feet

A desirable neighbourhood sits higher on the house price axis, as every price in this area exceeds those for the undesirable neighbourhood, and a slightly steeper curve is also apparent with the more desirable area. Putting these two factors together it appears that the desirable neighbourhood has a greater constant factor (α) and a greater slope factor (β), represented in the last section with intercept and interaction dummies respectively. However, despite their variations the question is if the two theoretical regression equations are similar enough, so that the differences are statistically or economically insignificant and the same regression model could suffice for both.

A Chow test can determine if there are differences between two hedonic regressions, the term used for the models estimated with observed data. The Chow test is a special form of a dummy variable test and model as it accounts for fluctuating data in a sample, without the need to construct intercept or interaction dummies. As usual with hypothesis testing the Chow test has a null hypothesis (H0) that the issue under investigation is insignificant, and in this example this means that there's no significant difference between the regression equation for a desirable neighbourhood's price (P_D), and that for an undesirable neighbourhood's price (P_{DU}):

$$H0: P_D i = P_{DU} i = \alpha i + \beta S i + \varepsilon i$$
$$H1: P_D i \neq P_{DU} i$$

If the null hypothesis were correct then the two sets of relevant sample data could be pooled and treat as one sample, but if the null hypothesis were rejected then the intercepts and slopes of the two sample regressions will differ and they can't be pooled. To test this null hypothesis a pooled equation would be estimated using the two samples together, to see if $\alpha_1 = \alpha_2$ and $\beta_1 = \beta_2$ or if one or both of these hypotheses are rejected and there's a significant difference between the samples. If the null hypothesis is rejected then the pooling of data will have essentially imposed constraints, or restrictions, which aren't true.

The Chow test may sound very similar to an F test examined earlier with a restricted and unrestricted model, and it's essentially the same test although used for a different purpose. Here the restrictions aren't based around the premise that additional variables are insignificant, but the premise that two data samples are equivalent and the difference between them is insignificant.

While the example with desirable and undesirable neighbourhoods is purely theoretical and relevant data is unavailable, it is possible to run through a Chow test using the data examined earlier on inflation and unemployment. This data has already been pooled into quarterly data for the years 1975-78, but perhaps it shouldn't have been, and maybe the first half for 1975-76 is statistically different to the years 1977-78. The data will be divided into two subsamples of eight observations to assess this restriction.

The Chow test is an F-test with the following formula:

$$F = [(rRSS - uRSS) / r] / [uRSS / n - k]$$

Letter n is the total number of observations which is 16 here, and k the total number of parameters in a model. The inflation model examined earlier had only one x variable (unemployment) which gives two parameters, but with the sample split in half in the unrestricted model there are now two models for a total of k = 4. Letter r represents the number of restricted parameters which is 2 here, as if the restriction is enforced and the data treat as one 1975-78 sample there are only 2 parameters, but without the restriction the data has two separate samples, 1975-76 and 1977-78, for a total of 4 parameters, and 4 - 2 = 2.

The rRSS or restricted residual sum of squares is already known, and the full sample of SE England quarterly unemployment and Retail Price Index inflation changes data enforces the restriction that the two subsamples are equivalent. Earlier tests on this full sample gave an RSS of 397.296, which is the rRSS here. Only one more value is required to perform a Chow test and that is the uRSS and the unrestricted residual sum of squares. This simply totals the RSS values for the two subsamples of 1975-76 and 1977-78, $uRSS = RSS_1 + RSS_2$.

Quarterly 1975-76 data includes 8 observations in the subsample, and an Excel regression on this gives RSS_1.

(1) y = 20.35, x = 2.0;
(2) y = 24.34, x = 2.5;
(3) y = 26.56, x = 2.8;
(4) y = 25.29, x = 3.4;
(5) y = 22.54, x = 3.7;
(6) y = 15.94, x = 3.9;
(7) y = 13.73, x = 4.0;
(8) y = 14.95, x = 4.0.

Residual
SS = 113.594

RSS_1 = 113.594, and another Excel regression on the 8 observations of quarterly 1977-78 data will give RSS_2.

(9) y = 16.50, x = 4.1;
(10) y = 17.41, x = 4.1;
(11) y = 16.50, x = 4.2;
(12) y = 13.01, x = 4.2;
(13) y = 9.44, x = 4.0;
(14) y = 7.71, x = 3.9;
(15) y = 7.88, x = 3.8;
(16) y = 8.13, x = 3.6.

Residual
SS = 49.8503

RSS_2 = 49.8503 here, which means RSS_1 + RSS_2 = 113.594 + 49.8503 = 163.4443 = uRSS. With this last value a Chow test can be performed to test the null hypothesis that there is no difference between the regression equations for 1975-76 and 1977-78 samples:

H0: 1975-76 regression = 1977-78 regression
H1: 1975-76 regression ≠ 1977-78 regression

The F-test is as follows:

$$F = [(rRSS - uRSS) / r] / [uRSS / n - k]$$
$$F = [(397.296 - 163.4443) / 2] / [163.4443 / 12]$$
$$F = 116.92585 / 13.620358$$
$$F = 8.5846$$

And this test result is compared with the test statistic critical value in the $F_{r, n-k}$ distribution tables, where the degrees of freedom of df1 = 2 and df2 = 12 give a critical value of 3.89 at a 5% significance level, and 6.93 at the 1% significance level. As the F test result exceeds these critical values we reject the null hypothesis that the 1975-76 and 1977-78 unemployment and inflation sample data are equivalent, and even at a strict 1% significance level (only 1% margin of error) the subsamples are found to be statistically different.

It appears that the 1975-78 data shouldn't be evaluated together as the relationship between unemployment and inflation changes significantly over the duration of the sample. This result could be predicted in advance with a quick look over the general trends in the two subsamples of 8 observations created here, and in the first one the x variable of unemployment rises over time as the inflation y variable falls, while in the second subsample the y variable again decreases but this time the x variable decreases with it.

This last example shows the potential applications of the Chow test, and not only can it be used to see if two separate samples can be pooled together, but it can also evaluate if one sample should be split into smaller ones to avoid giving potentially misleading results.

Heteroscedasticity

It has been assumed up to this point that the conditions required for a BLUE (best linear unbiased estimator) model and accurate hypothesis testing are met, but this section and the rest of this book addresses scenarios where a model's assumptions may break down and examines the effects that can result.

Consider a model where household food expenditure (y) is a function of household income (x):

$$y = \alpha + \beta x$$

Common sense may suggest that a function like this will be better at explaining household expenditure on food for lower income households than higher income ones. One theory may be that large proportions of lower levels of income (all poorer households have) for all people are likely to be spent on meeting basic food needs, while higher income levels may or may not go to food consumption depending on how important non-essential food is to a household. In simple terms lower income household food expenditure may be dependent solely on their income and what they can afford, while higher income household food expenditure may depend on other characteristic variables not included in this model.

The following data is a 40 observation sample of household income levels (x variable) and the corresponding household expenditure on food (y variable), and it allows an examination of the theory above.

(1) y = 52.25, x = 258.3;
(2) y = 58.32, x = 343.1;
(3) y = 81.79, x = 425;
(4) y = 119.9, x = 467.5;
(5) y = 125.8, x = 482.9;
(6) y = 100.46, x = 487.7;
(7) y = 121.51, x = 496.5;
(8) y = 100.08, x = 519.4;
(9) y = 127.75, x = 543.3;
(10) y = 104.94, x = 548.7;
(11) y = 107.48, x = 564.6;
(12) y = 98.48, x = 588.3;
(13) y = 181.21, x = 591.3;
(14) y = 122.23, x = 607.3;
(15) y = 129.57, x = 611.2;
(16) y = 92.84, x = 631;
(17) y = 117.92, x = 659.6;
(18) y = 82.13, x = 664;
(19) y = 182.28, x = 704.2;
(20) y = 139.13, x = 704.8;

(21) y = 98.14, x = 719.8;
(22) y = 123.94, x = 720;
(23) y = 126.31, x = 722.3;
(24) y = 146.47, x = 722.3;
(25) y = 115.98, x = 734.4;
(26) y = 207.23, x = 742.5;
(27) y = 119.8, x = 747.7;
(28) y = 151.33, x = 763.3;
(29) y = 169.51, x = 810.2;
(30) y = 108.03, x = 818.5;
(31) y = 168.9, x = 825.6;
(32) y = 227.11, x = 833.3;
(33) y = 84.94, x = 834;
(34) y = 98.7, x = 918.1;
(35) y = 141.06, x = 918.1;
(36) y = 215.4, x = 929.6;
(37) y = 112.89, x = 951.7;
(38) y = 166.25, x = 1014;
(39) y = 115.43, x = 1141.3;
(40) y = 269.03, x = 1154.6.

Key regression statistics for the 40 observation sample are as follows:

Coefficients
Intercept = 40.768
X variable 1 = 0.1283

Standard Error
Intercept = 22.139
X variable 1 = 0.0305

t Stat
Intercept = 1.8415
X variable 1 = 4.2008

P-value
Intercept = 0.0734
X variable 1 = 0.000155

The expected relationship between household food expenditure (y) and household income (x) is therefore:

$$y_i = 40.768 + 0.1283x$$

But dividing the intercept and x variable coefficients by their corresponding level of standard error, to give the t statistic Excel presents here, reveals that the intercept is not statistically significant at the 5% significance level. Its t statistic of 1.8415 is lower than the critical value at this level, and we don't even need to look at what the t table values are to know this as the intercept's p-value of 0.0734 is greater than 5% (i.e. 0.05). A significance level (margin of error) greater than 7.34% is required to reject the null hypothesis that the intercept equals zero and is statistically insignificant, which may be too large to be reliable and therefore the constant might be irrelevant here.

Even if the constant is kept in a model despite its irrelevance, which often occurs as removing may affect the influence of x variables and ruin the model, there are still problems with the regression equation after rearranging it in terms of expected error ($\underline{\varepsilon}i$):

$$\underline{\varepsilon}i = \underline{y}i - 40.768 - 0.1283x$$

No calculations or graphs need to be made to show that this model is unreliable, and a quick glance at the 40 observations used in this sample reveals its problems. The 40 observations above are arranged with ascending values of the x variable (household income), and the y variable (household food expenditure) rises with x at lower income values to give potentially constant expected error according to the equation above. But with higher income levels the y variable shows little if any correlation with x, and food expenditure jumps from roughly 100 to beyond 200 and then back again, which will cause the model's expected error to move around wildly. It appears that this model and household income are better at explaining household food expenditure (y) for those at lower income (x) levels than those with higher income levels, just as expected before the sample was examined.

Remember that the conditions needed for a best linear unbiased estimator (BLUE) included homoscedasticity:

1. The x variables are fixed on repeated sampling;
2. Expected individual error is zero, $E(\varepsilon i) = 0$;
3. Homoscedasticity or constant variance, $E(\varepsilon i^2) = \sigma^2$;
4. No autocorrelation, cov $(\varepsilon i, \varepsilon j) = 0$ with $i \neq j$.

Homoscedastic errors

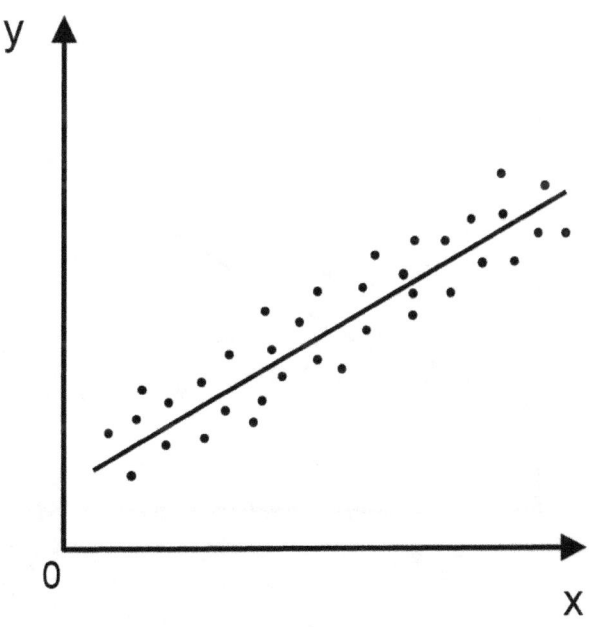

But the 40 observation sample of household income (x variable) against household food expenditure (y variable), which proxies the real relationship of these two variables in the population, doesn't follow the homoscedastic error pattern of constant variance from the regression equation (best fit line) in the diagram above. The trend instead is more like heteroscedastic error and non-constant variance.

Heteroscedastic errors

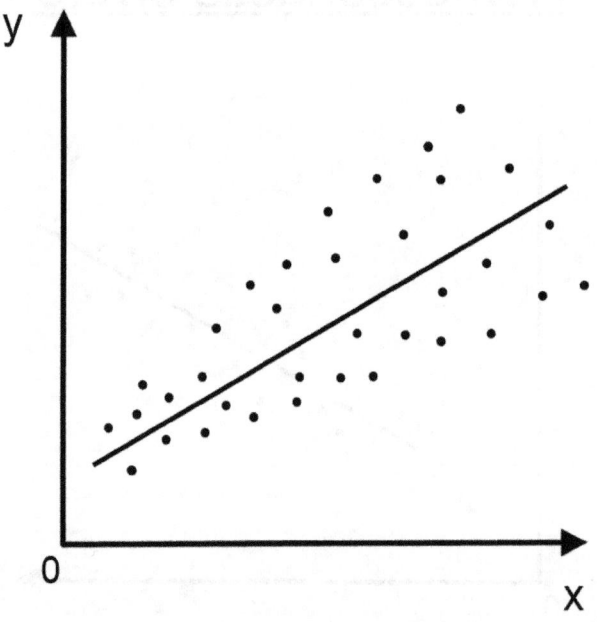

If heteroscedasticity exists as with this sample then the variance of a dependent variable observation, (var) y_i, and individual error term, (var) ε_i, is no longer fixed at σ^2 and instead will have its own individual value at σ_i^2. The random variable and random error are then both heteroscedastic. If this systematic pattern of non-constant variance exists in the errors then ordinary least squares (OLS) is challenged, as the method assumes efficiency with all observations equally reliable in error minimization. OLS is still a linear unbiased estimator even with heteroscedasticity, as unbiasedness only depends upon independent x variables and an expected mean error of zero, but efficiency is threatened and the model is no longer the best available.

To maintain model efficiency for accurate estimation and prediction observations will have to be reweighted to ensure there is equal error variance, with those observations with greater error variance weighted less to reduce it. However, standard errors of the estimates will be biased as standard error can't be reweighted, and biased standard errors prevent calculations of accurate confidence interval test statistics and create a model that will not be efficient. This means t statistics, F statistics and LM statistics can't be used to perform hypothesis tests as any inferences drawn from them may be wrong.

With homoscedasticity the formula for least squares, the lowest possible squared error, is as follows where Xi is an individual value from the data sample, $\overline{X}$ is the sample mean, and Xi - $\overline{X}$ = xi, with xi a value from the population that is being estimated:

$$\text{var}(\beta) = \sigma^2 / \sum (X_i - \bar{X})^2$$

But with heteroscedasticity this formula is wrong, and the correct formula for least squares becomes:

$$\text{var}(\beta) = \sum \sigma_i^2 (X_i - \bar{X})^2 / [\sum (X_i - \bar{X})^2]^2$$

This simply involves two changes to the original equation, and it first accounts for the non-constant variance and individual variance of every observation as σ_i^2 multiplied by x_i (i.e. $X_i - \bar{X}$) replaces constant σ^2, and second it squares and sums all parts of the OLS equation. But this equation relates to the real population variance which is unknown, and an estimator will be required to use with sample observations as a proxy.

Hal White offers an estimator that can approximate for the variance of the least squares estimator here, $\underline{\text{var}(\beta)}$, and this sees σ_i^2 in the equation above replaced with the estimator's squares of the least squares residuals, $\underline{\varepsilon}_i^2$:

$$\underline{\text{var}(\beta)} = \sum \underline{\varepsilon}_i^2 (X_i - \bar{X})^2 / [\sum (X_i - \bar{X})^2]^2$$

In large samples White's estimated standard error value, found with the square root of the estimated variance here, is an accurate and consistent measure and it will be unbiased with heteroscedastic data unlike the original standard error. But this only holds with large samples and it should not be used with small samples where the variance is typically larger at the mean (centre) of the distribution as opposed to the extremes (tails), and the distribution is more peaked. With smaller samples heteroscedasticity is unlikely to be significant enough to cause problems and there may not be a need to make model adjustments. In larger data samples the distribution will be more spread out with a shorter peak and fatter tails, representing a larger variance which the squared residuals of White's sample are designed to approximate.

Returning to the household expenditure data, the estimated regression equation remains the same as before:

$$\underline{y}i = 40.768 + 0.1283x$$

But White's variance formula gives different estimates for the variance of the intercept (α) and slope (β):

$$\underline{var(\alpha)} = 561.89$$
$$\underline{var(\beta)} = 0.0014569$$

Taking the square root of these estimates for the estimated standard error also gives different results:

(Original incorrect OLS) Standard Error
Intercept = 22.139
X variable 1 = 0.0305

(White) Standard Error
Intercept = 23.704
X variable 1 = 0.0382

Remember that the formula to test a hypothesis of an x variable (e.g. H0: $\beta = 0$, H1: $\beta \neq 0$) is:

$$(\hat{\beta} - \beta) / \underline{Se}(\hat{\beta}) \sim t_{(n-2)}$$

The parameter estimate minus its hypothesized value and divided by the estimate's standard error approximates a t distribution, and the test statistic found with this formula can be compared to those in t tables to assess a hypothesis. Results can be compared for both the original and White's standard errors to show the different effect White's corrected measure offers. In both cases the two-tailed t test critical value with n - 2 = 38 degrees of freedom and a 5% significance level (95% confidence level) is $\pm$ 2.024. But the confidence intervals are different:

Original and incorrect OLS: [0.067, 0.190]
White: [0.051, 0.206]

These are the values of β that will see the test statistic remain in the critical region to fail to reject the null hypothesis. For example, with the original standard error and a 0.067 value of β the result is:

$$(\hat{\beta} - \beta) / \underline{Se}(\hat{\beta}) \sim t_{(n-2)}$$
$$(0.1283 - 0.067) / 0.0305 \sim t_{(n-2)}$$
$$2.01 \sim t_{(n-2)}$$

This is within the critical region but a slightly lower value than 0.067 can push the test statistic outside it to reject the null hypothesis and change the test result. And using the 0.190 value with the original incorrect standard error gives a value at the other end of the critical region:

$$(0.1283 - 0.190) / 0.0305 \sim t_{(n-2)}$$
$$-2.023 \sim t_{(n-2)}$$

With the original incorrect OLS standard errors the confidence interval is smaller, and the β value can only be between 0.067 and 0.190 or the null hypothesis is rejected. These standard errors overstate the estimation's precision and create narrower confidence intervals than there should be. But with White's adjustment for heteroscedasticity greater variance is accepted and the confidence intervals are wider, as β can take on any value between 0.051 and 0.206 without rejecting the null hypothesis.

White's standard error correction method shows how heteroscedasticity, or non-constant variance, may be tolerated without it ruining a model but perhaps we don't want to tolerate the problem and we want a way to fix it.

There are two different ways to remove heteroscedasticity and first the type found in a regression must be identified.

Proportional heteroscedasticity is where the non-constant variance is a continuous function of a variable, for example with different consumption variance as income levels change as seen earlier. Partitioned heteroscedasticity is where the variance changes among different discrete categories or groups, for example with changing consumption variance by race or sex.

With proportional heteroscedasticity the non-constant variance of the errors, var $(\varepsilon_i) = \sigma_i^2$, is assumed to be directly proportional to the value of an x variable, x_i:

$$\sigma_i^2 = \sigma^2 x_i$$

And taking the square root of this gives the following:

$$\sigma_i = \sigma \sqrt{x_i}$$

Heteroscedasticity is eliminated if error is constant (σ for population standard deviation and σ^2 for variance) and doesn't change with different individual observations (σ_i or σ_i^2), and this formula shows that all that is required to achieve this goal is to divide by the square root of an individual x variable observation, $\sqrt{x_i}$. This transforms the original heteroscedastic regression model as follows:

Heteroscedastic: $y_i = \alpha + \beta x_i + \varepsilon_i$
Corrected: $y_i/\sqrt{x_i} = \alpha(1/\sqrt{x_i}) + \beta(x_i/\sqrt{x_i}) + \varepsilon_i/\sqrt{x_i}$

This corrected for heteroscedasticity model may be shortened, as the symbol * is used to represent $(/\sqrt{x_i})$:

$$y_i^* = \alpha x_{i_1}^* + \beta x_{i_2}^* + \varepsilon_i^*$$

And the variance of ε_i^* is:

$$\text{var}(\varepsilon_i^*) = \text{var}(\varepsilon_i/\sqrt{x_i}) = (1/x_i)\text{var}(\varepsilon_i) = (1/x_i)\sigma^2 x_i$$
$$\text{var}(\varepsilon_i^*) = \sigma^2$$

This shows that the method to divide by $(/\sqrt{x_i})$ is effective, and while ε_i is heteroscedastic ε_i^* is homoscedastic with constant variance σ^2. This generalized least squares (GLS), or weight least squares, method has three steps:

1. Determine which variable is proportional to the heteroscedastic errors (x_i in the last example);

2. Divide all factors in the original model by the square root of the relevant variable ($\sqrt{x_i}$ here);

3. Run a least squares regression on the transformed model with new y_i^*, $x_{i_1}^*$ and $x_{i_2}^*$ variables but no intercept ($y_i^* = \alpha x_{i_1}^* + \beta x_{i_2}^* + \varepsilon_i^*$ in the last example, where * represents $(/\sqrt{x_i})$).

Using the GLS measures on the 40 observation sample of household food expenditure against household income earlier gives a new regression equation, with new standard error values in brackets underneath each factor:

$$y_i = 31.924 + 0.1410x$$
$$(17.986) \quad (0.0270)$$

α and β mean the same thing in this transformed model as before but with GLS the intercept is smaller (31.926 instead of 40.768) and the slope larger (0.1410 instead of 0.1283) than the original heteroscedastic model. The standard errors are lower for both factors than before at 17.986 for the intercept (previously 22.139 with OLS and 23.704 for White), and 0.0270 for the slope (previously 0.0305 for OLS and 0.0382 for White).

As GLS is a better estimator (but more effort) than OLS the standard errors would be expected to be lower, while White's measure has the highest standard errors as it uses a wide confidence interval to cover for the inaccuracy caused by heteroscedasticity in place of removing it as GLS does. GLS and its smaller standard errors produce narrower, more informative confidence intervals compared to the other two methods, and with a 95% confidence level and $\pm$ 2.024 critical value the GLS range of possible values are [0.086, 0.196], instead of the OLS values of [0.067, 0.190] and White's least squares values [0.051, 0.206].

Partitioned heteroscedasticity sees a non-constant variance that varies by group, and within this group the variance is constant. For example, the usual regression model, $yi = \alpha + \beta xi + \varepsilon i$, may see yi represent the number of bushels of corn in a harvest, and xi represent the gallons of water per acre (via rain or watering etc.), where i ranges from 1 to 100. But the corn is partitioned into two different types, and when $i = 1,...,80$ it is 'field' corn with error variance, var $(\varepsilon i) = \sigma_1^2$, yet when $i = 81,...,100$ the corn is 'sweet' corn with error variance, var $(\varepsilon i) = \sigma_2^2$.

To resolve this heteroscedasticity the 3 steps noted for GLS must be applied, with each of the two group's observations reweighted accordingly. As the error variance of field corn is var $(\varepsilon i) = \sigma_1^2$ the regression equation must be divided by σ_1 for $i = 1,...,80$ observations:

$$yi/\sigma_1 = \alpha(1/\sigma_1) + \beta(xi/\sigma_1) + \varepsilon i/\sigma_1$$

With sweet corn's error variance at var $(\varepsilon i) = \sigma_2^2$ the equation is divided by σ_2 for $i = 81,...,100$ observations:

$$yi/\sigma_2 = \alpha(1/\sigma_2) + \beta(xi/\sigma_2) + \varepsilon i/\sigma_2$$

Least squares is then run separately on each group, with sample estimate $\underline{\sigma}_1^2$ an estimator for the population value σ_1^2 using the 80 field corn observations, and $\underline{\sigma}_2^2$ an estimator for σ_2^2 using the 20 sweet corn observations.

These examples show that once the existence and type of heteroscedasticity is known it can be resolved for a BLUE model. Residual plots in statistical software can help detect heteroscedasticity, where the residuals (error) from a regression are plotted against one x variable at a time to examine the relationship between the two, after data is sorted by ascending values of that variable. The diagram below shows what it may look like if proportional heteroscedasticity is found with xi.

Residual plots

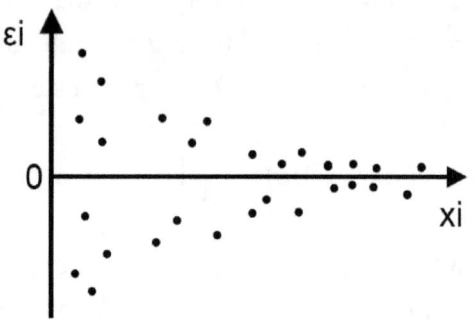

Another way to detect heteroscedasticity is with the Goldfeld-Quandt (GQ) test, and this can detect the proportional form and compare two groups with the partitioned form. It can be useful to use the residual plot method first to see if there appears to be non-constant variance with a variable, and then the GQ test can statistically determine if the heteroscedasticity is serious enough for changes to be required in the model.

With proportional heteroscedasticity the sample data of the affected variable is sorted into either ascending or descending order, so the start of the ordered data has the higher expected error, and the middle 'r' number of observations are usually dropped , where $r \approx n / 6$. Then separate least squares regressions are run on the first n_1 and last n_2 observations. The null hypothesis is that there's no heteroscedasticity and the two sets' variances are equal:

$$H0: \sigma_1^2 = \sigma_2^2$$
$$H1: \sigma_1^2 \neq \sigma_2^2$$

The GQ test statistic uses sample data estimates for the two variances and the result is assessed against the F table:

$$GQ = \underline{\sigma}_1^2 / \underline{\sigma}_2^2 \sim F_{(n1-k1, n2-k2)}$$

And n_1 and k_1 in the degrees of freedom are the number of observations and model parameters for the regression run on the first n_1 observations, and n_2 and k_2 are those for the second n_2 sample. If the GQ value is large enough it exceeds the F test's critical value and the null hypothesis is rejected to suggest heteroscedasticity.

Returning to the household expenditure and income data, with only 40 observations it's counterproductive to remove the middle $n/6$ and the sample data can simply be divided into two subsamples of 20 each, after arranging income values in descending order (for declining expected error here). The household data GQ test statistic value is:

$$GQ = 2285.9 / 682.46 = 3.35$$

And with a 5% significance level the $F_{(18, 18)}$ table critical value is 2.22. As the GQ test statistic is greater than this the null hypothesis is rejected, and the two subsample's variances are not equal and observation variance is not constant across the entire data sample, $\sigma_i^2 \neq \sigma^2$. Instead error variance depends upon the income level, $\sigma_i^2 = \sigma^2 x_i$, with proportional heteroscedasticity.

A Breusch-Pagan (BP) test detects heteroscedasticity in linear forms, and estimates error with residuals from the OLS regression. First this regresses the squared residuals on all x variables, with v_i the residual regression's error:

$$\underline{\varepsilon}_i^2 = \delta_0 + \delta_1 x_1 + \delta_2 x_2 + \ldots + \delta_k x_k + v_i$$

H0 is that all auxiliary regression variables equal zero:

$$H0: \delta_0 = \delta_1 = \delta_2 = \ldots = \delta_k = 0$$
H1: Not all parameters equal zero

The regression's R^2 is used for an F or LM test, and the LM test uses Chi-squared distribution χ^2. Letter k represents the no. of parameters in the auxiliary regression:

$$F = [R^2/k] / [(1 - R^2) / (n - k - 1)] \sim F_{(k, n-k-1)}$$
$$LM = nR^2 \sim \chi^2_k$$

The White test allows for nonlinearities using squares and cross products of all x variables, and there's no need to specify which x variable has heteroscedasticity. It again uses an F or LM test to test if all variables (x_j), squares (x_j^2) and cross products ($x_j x_h$) are jointly significant. The degrees of freedom k value is the number of regressors in the auxiliary equation, with all squares and cross products. Another form the White test regresses the squared residuals from the auxiliary regression on estimates $\underline{y}$ and $\underline{y}^2$, which are a function of all x variable squares and cross products, and the R^2 is used in the F or LM test.

Econometric or statistical software can easily calculate the Goldfeld-Quandt, Breusch-Pagan, or White test statistics, and this is the most efficient way to test for heteroscedasticity.

Autocorrelation

For model efficiency and accurate estimation all systematic information must be incorporated into the regression model. If a systematic pattern emerges in a regression's residual errors then this suggests that not all information is incorporated in the model, a situation known as autocorrelation which violates a condition of the BLUE (best linear unbiased estimator) model:

1. The x variables are fixed on repeated sampling;
2. Expected individual error is zero, $E(\varepsilon i) = 0$;
3. Homoscedasticity or constant variance, $E(\varepsilon i^2) = \sigma^2$;
4. <u>No autocorrelation, cov $(\varepsilon i, \varepsilon j) = 0$ with $i \neq j$.</u>

While the problem of heteroscedasticity sees regression error variance that changes with different values of an x variable as opposed to remaining constant, autocorrelation involves errors that are dependent on the value of other errors as opposed to being random. Autocorrelation may involve either errors that are systematically attracted to each other (positive autocorrelation) or systematically repelled by each other (negative autocorrelation). The following diagrams show the appearance of each of the two different types of autocorrelation in a regression's residuals, before the third diagram shows a situation of no autocorrelation.

Positive auto.

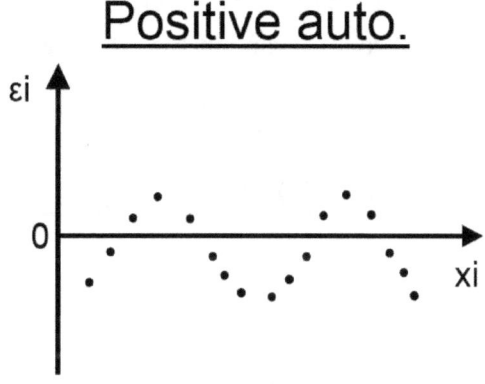

Negative auto.

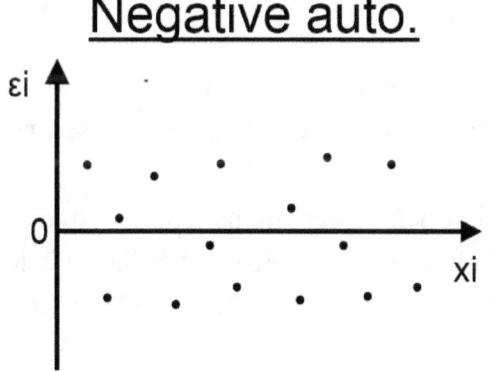

With positive autocorrelation errors don't cross the expected zero error line enough, and with negative auto. they cross too much. With no autocorrelation errors should cross the line of zero error randomly with no covariance.

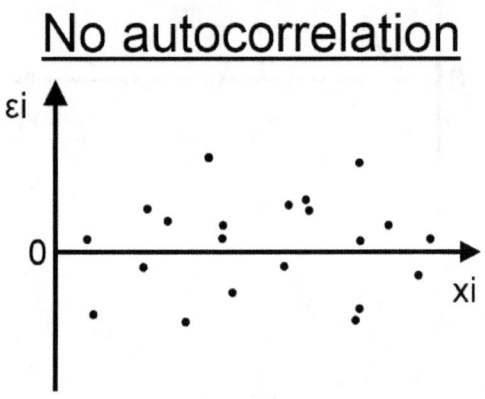

First order autocorrelation sees an observation's error affected by the last observation's error, second order by the last two errors, etc. This situation is easiest to understand when observations change over time, and autocorrelation relates to error (ε) being affected by past error (ε_t), with correlation coefficient ρ between -1 and 1:

$$1^{st} \text{ order: } \varepsilon_t = \rho\varepsilon_{t-1} + v_t$$
$$2^{nd} \text{ order: } \varepsilon_t = \rho_1\varepsilon_{t-1} + \rho_2\varepsilon_{t-2} + v_t$$
$$3^{rd} \text{ order: } \varepsilon_t = \rho_1\varepsilon_{t-1} + \rho_2\varepsilon_{t-2} + \rho_3\varepsilon_{t-3} + v_t$$

For the time being only first order autocorrelation will be examined, denoted as AR(1): $\varepsilon_t = \rho\varepsilon_{t-1} + v_t$. The term v_t represents the error of the error term's equation, and all of the usual assumptions of an expected zero mean value, homoscedasticity and constant variance (σ_v^2 here), and no autocorrelation are assumed with this. These assumptions about v_t imply the following holds for ε_t:

$$E(\varepsilon_t) = 0$$
$$var(\varepsilon_t) = \sigma_\varepsilon^2 = \sigma_v^2 / (1 - \rho^2)$$
$$cov\ (\varepsilon_t, \varepsilon_{t-k}) = \sigma_\varepsilon^2\rho^k \text{ for } k > 0$$
$$corr\ (\varepsilon_t, \varepsilon_{t-k}) = \rho^k \text{ for } k > 0$$

With autocorrelation the least squares estimator is still linear and unbiased but not efficient, as errors will linger to give misleading results. Formulas used to calculate least squares standard errors will be incorrect and confidence intervals and hypothesis tests using them will be wrong.

Autocorrelation is best demonstrated with an example, and the following 34 data observations examine the area of sugar cane planted in a region of Bangladesh, the country in SE Asia. The dependent y variable is the area planted (A), and the independent x variable is the output price (P) thought to motivate and explain it.

(1) A = 29, P = 0.075258;
(2) A = 71, P = 0.114894;

(3) A = 42, P = 0.101075;

(4) A = 90, P = 0.110309;

(5) A = 72, P = 0.109562;

(6) A = 57, P = 0.132486;

(7) A = 44, P = 0.141783;

(8) A = 61, P = 0.209559;

(9) A = 60, P = 0.188259;

(10) A = 70, P = 0.195946;

(11) A = 88, P = 0.226087;

(12) A = 80, P = 0.145585;

(13) A = 125, P = 0.19403;

(14) A = 232, P = 0.270362;

(15) A = 125, P = 0.235821;

(16) A = 99, P = 0.220826;

(17) A = 250, P = 0.380952;

(18) A = 91, P = 0.205394;

(19) A = 121, P = 0.267396;

(20) A = 162, P = 0.230411;

(21) A = 143, P = 0.368771;

(22) A = 138, P = 0.285076;

(23) A = 230, P = 0.360332;

(24) A = 128, P = 0.322976;

(25) A = 87, P = 0.301266;

(26) A = 124, P = 0.287834;

(27) A = 97, P = 0.401437;

(28) A = 152, P = 0.404692;

(29) A = 197, P = 0.353188;

(30) A = 220, P = 0.410233;
(31) A = 171, P = 0.360418;
(32) A = 208, P = 0.463087;
(33) A = 237, P = 0.401582;
(34) A = 235, P = 0.39166.

However, the x variable (P) data observations are a tiny fraction of the y variable (A) observations, which may cause issues with the regression by creating very large coefficient and residual values. To make data such as this more manageable it's a good idea to take natural logs of the variables, replacing the linear model with a log-log model that assumes constant elasticity:

$$Ln\ (A_t) = \alpha + \beta\ Ln\ (P_t) + \varepsilon_t$$

And Ln (A_t) can be denoted as y_t while Ln (P_t) can be denoted as x_t, to write the equation as $y_t = \alpha + \beta x_t + \varepsilon_t$. The change of data can easily be done in Excel, with the creation of two new columns y and x, and their data values follow the formulas '$= Ln(A_t)$' and '$= Ln(P_t)$' respectively. With a log-log regression the estimated equation is as follows, with standard errors in brackets and R^2 also noted:

$$y_t = 6.111 + 0.971x_t$$
$$(0.169)\ (0.111)$$
$$R^2 = 0.706$$

However, plotting the regressions residuals in a graph reveals a pattern of what appears to be autocorrelation, with both positive and negative autocorrelation trends visible in the error observations. This would make the standard errors just noted incorrect and create a model that can't be accurately tested. To resolve this potential problem the model needs to account for the possible presence of autocorrelation (assumed to be AR(1) only as this is the most common):

$$y_t = \alpha + \beta x_t + \varepsilon_t$$
$$AR(1): \varepsilon_t = \rho \varepsilon_{t-1} + v_t$$
$$y_t = \alpha + \beta x_t + \rho \varepsilon_{t-1} + v_t$$

But although the amended model now accounts for autocorrelation a regression can't calculate ε_{t-1}, and this variable needs to be replaced before a regression can proceed. This can be done by rearranging the original model (before autocorrelation AR(1) was added) in terms of ε_t and then lagging the errors once, so t becomes t-1:

$$\varepsilon_t = y_t - \alpha - \beta x_t$$
$$\varepsilon_{t-1} = y_{t-1} - \alpha - \beta x_{t-1}$$

Then this can replace the problematic ε_{t-1} in the amended model before the equation is simplified in steps:

$$y_t = \alpha + \beta x_t + \rho (y_{t-1} - \alpha - \beta x_{t-1}) + v_t$$
$$y_t = \alpha + \beta x_t + \rho y_{t-1} - \rho\alpha - \rho\beta x_{t-1} + v_t$$
$$y_t - \rho y_{t-1} = \alpha(1 - \rho) + \beta(x_t - \rho x_{t-1}) + v_t$$

This can then be rewritten in a more simple form:

$$y_t{}^* = \alpha^* + \beta x_t{}^* + v_t$$

Where $y_t{}^*$, $x_t{}^*$, and α^* are as follows:

$$y_t{}^* = y_t - \rho y_{t-1}$$
$$x_t{}^* = x_t - \rho x_{t-1}$$
$$\alpha^* = \alpha(1 - \rho)$$

But although this model can be tested in a regression there are two problems estimating it with least squares, as one observation is used up creating the lagged variables leaving only n - 1 to estimate the model, while the value of ρ is not known and an estimation method is required.

Dropping the first observation (to use as a lagged variable) and applying least squares is not the best linear unbiased estimation (BLUE) method. As the observations are not all put through the same process the variance of the first observation's error is not equal to that of the other errors, and efficiency is lost. This situation is a special case of the heteroscedasticity problem, as all error variance is assumed equal except for the first observation.

A method is required to recover the first (1) observation, and it could be recovered as it was dropped:

$$y_1 = \alpha + \beta x_1 + \varepsilon_1$$
$$\text{var}(\varepsilon_1) = \sigma_\varepsilon^2 = \sigma_v^2 / (1 - \rho^2)$$

However, the other observations in the y_t^* regression have error variance of σ_v^2 and the error variance of ε_1 must be transformed from σ_ε^2 to match this or the model will include heteroscedasticity. Given a constant factor, c, the following will hold:

$$\text{var}(c\ \varepsilon_1) = c^2\ \text{var}(\varepsilon_1)$$

And if $c = \sqrt{(1 - \rho^2)}$ then:

$$\text{var}(\sqrt{(1 - \rho^2)}\ \varepsilon_1) = (1 - \rho^2)\ \text{var}(\varepsilon_1)$$
$$= (1 - \rho^2)\ \sigma_\varepsilon^2$$
$$= (1 - \rho^2)\ \sigma_v^2 / (1 - \rho^2)$$
$$= \sigma_v^2$$

Transformed error $v_1 = \sqrt{(1 - \rho^2)}\ \varepsilon_1$ has variance σ_v^2, which gives the recovered first observation the same error variance as the other n - 1 for a full set of n observations:

$$\sqrt{(1 - \rho^2)}\ y_1 = \sqrt{(1 - \rho^2)}\ \alpha + \sqrt{(1 - \rho^2)}\ \beta x_1 + \sqrt{(1 - \rho^2)}\ \varepsilon_1$$

However, this result comes back to the other problem noted, and how to estimate unknown value ρ. If ε_t and ε_{t-1} estimates were known then ρ could be estimated accordingly:

$$\varepsilon_t = \rho \, \varepsilon_{t-1} + v_t$$

This has be done in two steps and first least squares is used to estimate the model $y_t = \alpha + \beta x_t + \varepsilon_t$, where the estimated residuals are: $\underline{\varepsilon}_t = y_t - \alpha - \beta x_t$. With these residuals least squares can estimate: $\underline{\varepsilon}_t = \rho \, \underline{\varepsilon}_{t-1} + \underline{v}_t$, where the underlined feature represents an estimation as before. This gives the following least squares estimate for ρ:

$$\underline{\rho} = \sum \underline{\varepsilon}_t \, \underline{\varepsilon}_{t-1} / \sum \underline{\varepsilon}_{t-1}^2$$

With an estimator found for ρ and a recovered first observation given equal variance to the others, a regression model can be found which accounts for autocorrelation in the sugar cane data. First the value of $\underline{\rho}$ can be estimated from the data:

$$\underline{\rho} = \sum \underline{\varepsilon}_t \, \underline{\varepsilon}_{t-1} / \sum \underline{\varepsilon}_{t-1}^2 = 0.342$$

Then this estimated value can be used to change the observations to their * and transformed form, for example:

$$y_1^* = \sqrt{(1 - \rho^2)}\, y_1$$
$$y_1^* = \sqrt{(1 - 0.342^2)}\, (0.3673)$$
$$y_1^* = 3.1642$$

$$x_3^* = x_3 - \rho x_2$$
$$x_3^* = -2.2919 - (0.342)(-2.1637)$$
$$x_3^* = -1.5519$$

Where is y_1 is $Ln(A_1)$ from the data given above (i.e. Ln 29), and x_3 is $Ln(P_3)$ from the data (i.e. Ln 0.101075) and x_2 is $Ln(P_2)$ from the data (i.e. Ln 0.114894). Applying least squares to all weighted and transformed observations gives the generalized least squares (GLS) estimated model, with the original OLS model underneath as a comparison:

$$Ln\,(A_t) = 6.164 + 1.007\,Ln\,(P_t)$$
$$\text{GLS Se: } (0.213)\ (0.137)$$

$$Ln\,(A_t) = 6.111 + 0.971\,Ln\,(P_t)$$
$$\text{OLS Se: } (0.169)\ (0.111)$$

The method explained here creates a model which accounts for autocorrelation, but before these changes are made a statistical test for autocorrelation should be performed to determine if they are genuinely required.

There are three tests for autocorrelation, a Durbin-Watson (DW) test, Durbin h-test, and Breusch-Godfrey LM test.

A DW test uses the value of correlation coefficient ρ to test a null hypothesis that there's no autocorrelation in a model, with the DW test statistic known as d:

$$H0: \rho = 0$$
$$H1: \rho \neq 0$$

$$d = \sum (\varepsilon_t - \varepsilon_{t-1})^2 / \sum \varepsilon_t^2$$

The DW test has the following assumptions: the constant term is included, explanatory x variables are fixed on repeated sampling (i.e. independent), there are no lagged dependent variables, any autocorrelation follows an AR(1) trend only, and error term v_t is normally distributed. The test statistic, d, approximates to correlation coefficient estimate ρ as follows, where ρ is between -1 and 1:

$$d \approx 2(1 - \rho)$$

When $\rho = 0$ (no autocorrelation) $d \approx 2$, when $\rho = 1$ (perfect positive auto.) $d \approx 0$, and when $\rho = -1$ (perfect negative auto.) $d \approx 4$. The d value is then compared to those in the d tables, and the number of observations (n), number of explanatory variables excluding the constant term (k), and significance level decide two critical values,

D_L and D_U, the lower and upper bound values respectively. These affect the result of the hypothesis test as follows:

0 to D_L = Reject H0, positive autocorrelation;
D_L to D_U = Zone of indecision (i.e. fail to reject H0);
D_U to 4-D_U = Fail to reject H0;
4-D_U to 4-D_L = Zone of indecision (fail to reject H0);
4-D_L to 4 = Reject H0, negative autocorrelation.

However, tables of D_L and D_U critical values may not be readily available and it's easier to use the p-value of the DW test calculated with statistical software. If the p-value is lower than the chosen significance level (e.g. 0.05 for a 5% significance level) then the null hypothesis is rejected, but if the p-value is not lower then fail to reject the null hypothesis.

Although the DW test is useful it makes several restrictive assumptions as noted earlier, and assumes an intercept in the model, non-stochastic (non-random) x variable values, AR(1) disturbances, and no lagged dependent variables as an explanatory variable. The Durbin h-test changes this last assumption, and can deal with lagged dependent variables as explanatory factors in a model. The Durbin h formula is:

$$h = \rho \sqrt{(n \, / \, 1 - n \, \underline{var}(\beta 3))}$$

Where ρ is the correlation coefficient and estimated first-order autocorrelation, and $\underline{var}(\beta 3)$ is the estimated variance of the lagged variable coefficient. The h-test result can be calculated easily using regression statistics, and only the DW test d value and lagged variable standard error value are required. For example, a theoretical regression may give the following statistics:

$$y_t = 2.78 + 0.91x_1 - 0.55x_2 + 0.15y_{t-1}$$
$$\text{Se values: } (0.15) \ (0.23) \ (0.14)$$
$$\text{DW} = 1.8$$
$$n = 50$$

And from this data the value of $\underline{var}(\beta 3)$ and ρ can be found for the h-test formula:

$$\underline{var}(\beta 3) = 0.14^2 = 0.0196$$

$$d \approx 2(1 - \rho) \rightarrow \rho \approx 1 - 0.5d$$
$$\rho \approx 1 - 0.5 \ (1.8) \approx 0.1$$

$$h = \rho \ \sqrt{(n \ / \ 1 - n \ \underline{var}(\beta 3))}$$
$$h = 0.1 \ \sqrt{(50 \ / \ 1 - 50 \ (0.0196))}$$
$$h = 5.0$$

Even with a stringent 1% significance level the critical value in the h-test table is 2.576, far below the calculated h value of 5 here. Therefore the null hypothesis H0: $\rho = 0$ is rejected and the model in this example includes autocorrelation.

If the value of (n $\underline{\text{var}}(\beta)$) > 1 then the h-test is not applicable, as this would see the test have to take a square root of a negative number which is not possible. In this scenario Durbin has an alternative test, which first sees the following equation estimated with OLS:

$$y_t = \alpha + \beta_1 x_t + \beta_2 y_{t-1} + \varepsilon_t$$

This regression's residuals are then computed for another regression equation, where the hypothesis test for $\rho = 0$ is carried out by testing the significant of the ε_{t-1} coefficient (e.g. β_3) with a t test:

$$\varepsilon_t = \alpha + \beta_1 x_t + \beta_2 y_{t-1} + \beta_3 \varepsilon_{t-1}$$

A Breusch-Godfrey (BG) LM test includes lagged dependent variables and also tests higher orders of autocorrelation above 1st order AR(1):

1. Estimate the regression equation with OLS (e.g. $y_t = \alpha + \beta_1 x_{1t} + \beta_2 x_{2t} + \beta_3 y_{t-1} + \varepsilon_t$) and compute the residuals, ε_t;

2. Estimate the auxiliary regression model based on tested order of autocorrelation. (e.g. 2nd order has H0: $\rho_1 = \rho_2 = 0$, H1: at least one $\rho \neq 0$, with the auxiliary regression $\varepsilon_t = \alpha + \beta_1 x_{1t} + \beta_2 x_{2t} + \beta_3 y_{t-1} + \rho_1 \varepsilon_{t-1} + \rho_2 \varepsilon_{t-2} + v_t$);

3. For large sample sizes the test statistic is as follows, where p is the order of autocorrelation being tested:

$$(n - p)R^2 \sim \chi^2_p$$

With $p = 1$ the BG test is essentially a Durbin h-test;

4. If the calculated test statistic exceeds the critical chi-square value then reject the null hypothesis of no autocorrelation in any of the ρ terms.

Statistical software can test for (AR) 1-5 over the last five periods, and additional lag lengths for dependent variables may also be added. With computations a chi-square and F test result will often be presented and the latter may be used with smaller sample sizes.

If autocorrelation is found in a model then the current period's error can be used to estimate and predict future (t+1) outcomes. For example, with AR(1) autocorrelation:

$$y_{t+1} = \alpha + \beta x_{t+1} + \rho \varepsilon_t$$

And for n periods ahead the model would be:

$$y_{t+n} = \alpha + \beta x_{t+n} + \rho^n \varepsilon_t$$

If $\rho < 1$, then the influence of the error term will decrease the further into the future the equation examines.

Functional Form and Normality Tests

Omitting relevant variables or including irrelevant variables can be a problem when estimating an economic model. For example, a wage rate for a worker W_t may depend on their experience E_t and their motivation M_t:

$$W_t = \alpha + \beta_1 E_t + \beta_2 M_t + \varepsilon_t$$

However, data on motivation may not be available and therefore the model has to be estimated without it:

$$W_t = \alpha + \beta_1 E_t + \varepsilon_t$$

But this model is enforcing the restriction that $\beta_2 = 0$ when it isn't. Omitting this relevant variable will create a biased estimator, although it will have lower variance. This doesn't mean that the best strategy is to include as many variables as possible in a model to avoid this bias however, as this can also cause inaccuracy in a model. Perhaps instead of a wage rate equation excluding the motivation variable it includes an additional variable, P_t, which represents how many pets a worker has at home:

$$W_t = \alpha + \beta_1 E_t + \beta_2 M_t + \beta_3 P_t + \varepsilon_t$$

But in reality $\beta_3 = 0$ and the number of pets a worker has will have no effect on their wage rate, and P_t is an irrelevant variable. Including it here won't make the estimator biased but will increase the error and variances of all estimates to reduce the model's efficiency.

The Ramsey RESET test (Regression Specification Error Test), or RR test, detects both omitted variables and incorrect functional form, with misspecification of a variable a special type of functional form error. For example, a certain regression equation may be estimated:

$$y_t = \alpha + \beta_1 x_{1t} + \beta_2 x_{2t} + \varepsilon_t$$

But another model may also be under consideration with an additional variable, such as the estimate of the dependent variable squared:

$$y_t = \alpha + \beta_1 x_{1t} + \beta_2 x_{2t} + \gamma y_t^2 + \varepsilon_t$$

The RR test can test this model for misspecification:

$$H0: \gamma = 0$$
$$H1: \gamma \neq 0$$

And a higher order RR test could involve:

$$y_t = \alpha + \beta_1 x_{1t} + \beta_2 x_{2t} + \gamma_1 \underline{y}_t^2 + \gamma_2 \underline{y}_t^3 + \varepsilon_t$$

$$H0: \gamma_1 = \gamma_2 = 0$$
$$H1: \gamma_1 \neq 0 \text{ or } \gamma_2 \neq 0$$

Rejection of an RR null hypothesis implies that the original model was inadequate and can be improved with the additional variable(s), and shows that the original model had an omitted variable. But a failure to reject implies that the variable under consideration is an irrelevant variable and should not be included. The RR test focuses on powers of the original predictions of a model (i.e. y_t), based on the idea that if these artificial additions improve the model then it was flawed to begin with.

RR tests can be performed on both linear and log-log versions of a model using statistical packages, and as with other tests the p-value will give a quick answer to the hypothesis test above using F tables. If the p-value is below the chosen significance level then the null hypothesis is rejected, which means the original model is inadequate and the amended form model an improvement.

Although not one of the conditions for a BLUE model, normality is a condition required to test a hypothesis on a model as noted earlier:

<u>5. Error is normally distributed, $\varepsilon \sim N(0, \sigma^2)$</u>

Normal distribution

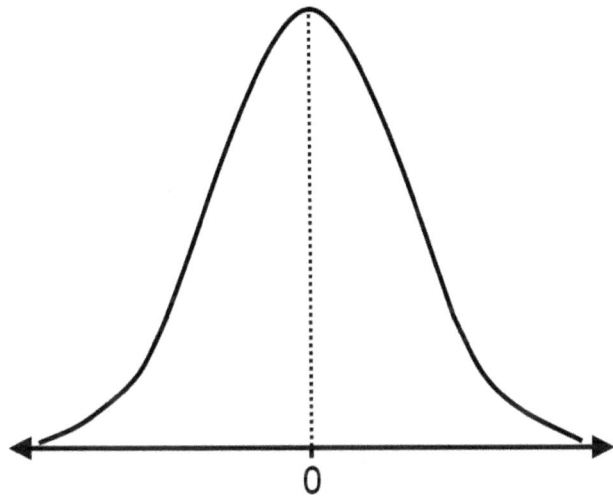

0

A normal distribution should look something like the diagram above and have a mean of 0 and variance σ^2, and to test whether the errors are normally distributed the residuals (i.e. errors) from a regression can be plotted in a histogram to see how they compare to the expected bell shape form. If they look nothing like this diagram then it's likely that they aren't normally distributed.

A more precise measure to test the normality of a model's errors is the Jarque-Bera (JB) test. This examines a model's symmetry and tests for skewness of 0 (perfect symmetry as in the diagram above instead of asymmetry), and also tests for kurtosis of 3 (peakedness and tails as in the diagram instead of being more peaked or flatter).

Skewness of 0 depends on the following equation of expected cubed error divided by cubed variance:

$$E(\varepsilon i^3) / \sigma^3 = 0$$

And this equation and the skewness level (S) can be estimated using error and variance estimates:

$$S = (1/\underline{\sigma}^3 n) \sum \varepsilon i^3$$

Kurtosis of 3 depends on the following equation of expected error to power four divided by variance to power four:

$$E(\varepsilon i^4) / \sigma^4 = 3$$

And this equation and the kurtosis level (K) can be estimated using error and variance estimates:

$$K = (1/\underline{\sigma}^4 n) \sum \varepsilon i^4$$

It can be shown that for large n values (large data samples):

$$S \sim N\ (0,\ 6/n)$$

$$K \sim N \ (3, 24/n)$$

This says that skewness has a mean of 0 and variance of 6/n, while kurtosis has a mean of 3 and variance of 24/n. These equations can be transformed to:

$$S \ / \ \sqrt{(6/n)} \sim N \ (0, 1)$$
$$K\text{-}3 \ / \ \sqrt{(24/n)} \sim N \ (0, 1)$$

This can then be tested with the null hypothesis, H0: zero skewness and normal kurtosis, using the JB test statistic:

$$JB = n \ [(S^2 \ / \ (6/n)) + ((K\text{-}3)^2 \ / \ (24/n))] \sim \chi^2_2$$

This can be computed with econometric software and H0 is rejected if the JB test statistic exceeds the χ^2_2 value at the chosen significance level, or if the computed p-value is lower than this significance level. If H0 is rejected then the assumption of a normal distribution doesn't hold with the model.

Method of Moments

There are six assumptions made in an econometric model, of which two are optional (5. Normally distributed errors, and 6. No perfect collinearity between variables in a multiple regression model). For the linear regression model of $y_i = \alpha + \beta x_i + \varepsilon_i$ with a single independent x variable there are four assumptions required for an efficient and unbiased (i.e. BLUE) estimator:

 1. The x variables are fixed on repeated sampling;
 2. Expected individual error is zero, $E(\varepsilon_i) = 0$;
 3. Homoscedasticity or constant variance, $E(\varepsilon_i^2) = \sigma^2$;
 4. No autocorrelation, cov $(\varepsilon_i, \varepsilon_j) = 0$ with $i \neq j$.

This section challenges the first assumption that x variables are fixed on repeated sampling. In the analytical and not experimental world of an economist x and y variables are revealed together, and this makes both variable types just as random as each other. This changes the assumptions of the linear model:

Both x_i and y_i are obtained randomly by sampling, and (as before) x_i must take at least two different values;

$E(\varepsilon|x) = 0$. Expected error, conditional on any value of x, is zero;

Var $(\varepsilon|x) = \sigma^2$. The error variance, conditional on any value of x, is constant at σ^2;

$\epsilon|x = \sim N\ (0, \sigma^2)$. The distribution of error, conditional on any value of x, is normal.

There is no mention of no autocorrelation here, as these modified assumptions assume it implicitly. The condition $E(\epsilon|x) = 0$ implies that no important variables have been omitted and the functional form is correct (or the model would have expected error), and there is nothing that causes the error term to be correlated with an x variable (i.e. no autocorrelation) as cov $(x, \epsilon) = 0$.

With small data samples and the assumption x is random the ordinary least squares (OLS) estimator remains BLUE, as the best linear unbiased estimator of the regression parameters. Estimators have a normal distribution and their variances are estimated as usual. This allows for accurate hypothesis testing and confidence interval calculation to proceed as before.

With large samples the probability distributions of the least squares estimators collapse around the true parameters β and σ, and estimation will be increasingly inaccurate. However, parameter estimators will be consistent in their inaccuracy with large samples (e.g. all x_1 values will be below the true value, or all x_2 values above its true value), and consistent parameter estimators can be useful with large samples.

But if explanatory variable estimations consistently have error there is an errors-in-variables problem, which sees the explanatory variable correlated with the error term. This creates inconsistency in the least squares estimator in measuring the regression model overall.

A worker's wage equation may be an example of the error-in-variables problem. In reality a worker's wages (y_i) may depend on their ability (x^*_i) as follows:

$$y_i = \alpha + \beta x^*_i + \varepsilon_i$$

But with a worker's true ability very difficult or impossible to know for sure an ability measure will likely contain error and a proxy measure is required. One possible proxy variable is a worker's performance on a standardized test. Their test score can be represented by variable x_i which is equal to their ability x^*_i and random error term u_i, where u_i has a 0 mean and variance σ_u^2 and is independently distributed and independent of ε_i:

$$x_i = x^*_i + u_i$$

Substituting x_i into the wage equation gives:

$$y_i = \alpha + \beta(x_i - u_i) + \varepsilon_i$$
$$y_i = \alpha + \beta x_i + (\varepsilon_i - \beta u_i)$$
$$y_i = \alpha + \beta x_i + v_i$$

In order to use least squares to estimate this equation it must first be determined whether or not x_i is correlated with random disturbance term vi, and if it is then this equation will also suffer from error-in-variables.

$$\text{cov}(xi, vi) = E(xivi) = E[(x^*i + ui)(\varepsilon i - \beta ui)$$
$$= E(-\beta ui^2) = -\beta\sigma_u^2 \neq 0$$

The least squares estimator is again an inconsistent estimator of β due to correlation between the explanatory x variable and error term, shown with the non-zero covariance above. $-\beta\sigma_u^2$ can't equal zero as β won't be zero as it's the only explanatory factor, while variance σ_u^2 won't be zero either as there will naturally be some error variance.

But a solution is available to the inconsistent estimator problem. Method of moment's estimators are consistent in large samples (where problems arise with random x variables), although they may not be the best or most efficient estimation method. The k'th moment of a random variable is that variable's expected value raised to the k'th power:

$$E(y^k) = \mu_k = \text{k'th moment of y}$$

And the real k'th population moment can be estimated consistently with a data sample of n size using formula:

$$\underline{E}(y^k) = \underline{\mu}_k = \text{k'th sample moment of y}$$

$$= \sum yi^k / n$$

The method of moments procedure has an m-estimator which equates m population moments to m sample moments to estimate m unknown parameters. Assume y is a random variable with mean of $E(y) = \mu$ and variance of $var(y) = \sigma^2 = E(y - \mu)^2 = E(y^2) - \mu^2$. To estimate the two real population parameters of μ and σ^2 the two population moments are equated to two sample moments. The first two population (μ) and sample estimate ($\underline{\mu}$) moments for y are as follows, where $\overline{Y}$ is the sample mean:

$$\mu_1 = E(y); \ \underline{\mu}_1 = \sum yi / n = \overline{Y}$$
$$\mu_2 = E(y^2); \ \underline{\mu}_2 = \sum yi^2 / n = \overline{Y}^2$$

Replacing the second population moment given above with its sample value reveals the estimated variance for the second moment, to show the process:

$$\underline{\sigma}^2 = \underline{E}(y^2) - \underline{\mu}^2$$
$$= (\sum yi^2 / n) - \overline{Y}^2 = (\sum yi^2 - n\overline{Y}^2) / n$$
$$= \sum (yi - \overline{Y})^2 / n$$

With the linear regression model $yi = \alpha + \beta xi + \varepsilon i$ it's assumed $E(\varepsilon i) = 0$, and if xi is fixed or random but not correlated with εi then $E(xi \varepsilon i) = 0$. This gives $E[xi(yi - \alpha - \beta xi)] = 0$. $E(.)$ relates to the population moments while form $\sum(.)/n$ gives the sample movements, and replacing the former with the latter for the two population moments gives two equations in two unknowns, for the method of moment's estimators for α; $1/n\sum (y_i - \underline{\alpha} - \underline{\beta}x_i)] = 0$, and β; $1/n\sum x_i(y_i - \underline{\alpha} - \underline{\beta}x_i)] = 0$.

But problems arise if x is random and correlated with the error term ε (as assumed in this section) so $E(x_i\varepsilon_i) \neq 0$. However, there may be another variable, z_i, known as an instrumental variable. And z_i may overcome the problem of x being correlated with error if it follows the required moment condition, $E(z_i\varepsilon_i) = 0$, $E[z_i(y_i - \alpha - \beta x_i)] = 0$. This gives the following method of moment's estimators for α (first equation) and β (second):

$$1/n\sum (y_i - \underline{\alpha} - \underline{\beta}x_i)] = 0$$
$$1/n\sum z_i(y_i - \underline{\alpha} - \underline{\beta}x_i)] = 0$$

Solving these gives what are known as instrumental variable estimators, where z is regressed instead of x:

$$\underline{\alpha} = \cancel{Y} - \underline{\beta}\cancel{X}$$
$$\underline{\beta} = (\sum z_i\sum y_i - n\sum z_iy_i) / (\sum z_i\sum x_i - n\sum z_ix_i)$$
$$= (z_i - \cancel{Z})(y_i - \cancel{Y}) / (z_i - \cancel{Z})(x_i - \cancel{X})$$

In large samples the sample covariance converges to the true covariance, and the instrumental variable estimator has an approximately normal distribution.

A Hausman test can determine if x is correlated with ε (a test for endogeneity). This has the null hypothesis that there is no correlation:

$$H0: \text{cov}(x, \varepsilon) = 0$$
$$H1: \text{cov}(x, \varepsilon) \neq 0$$

The test compares the performance of the least squares estimator with the instrumental (z) variables estimator. The model is first estimated with least squares, a process repeated for each x variable suspected to correlate with error, before the residuals, vi, are obtained:

$$xi = \alpha + \beta_1 zi_1 + \beta_2 zi_2 + vi$$
$$\underline{v}i = xi - \underline{\alpha} - \underline{\beta_1} zi_1 - \underline{\beta_2} zi_2$$

Next the computed residuals are included as an explanatory variable in a regression:

$$yi = \alpha + \beta xi + \delta \underline{v}i + \varepsilon i$$

And this artificial regression is estimated with least squares, with a t test to test the hypothesis for variable significance, or F test joint hypothesis if more than one suspected x variable. H0 is that $\delta = 0$, for no correlation between x and ε, and H1 is that $\delta \neq 0$, there is correlation.